Finding Peace Within

Part I
THE WAY TO CHRIST
by E. G. White

Part II
THE CHRISTIAN WAY
by L. Munilla and C. E. Wheeling

IBE, INC. • BOX 352 • JEMISON, AL 35085

Finding Peace Within
Part I – THE WAY TO CHRIST
was originally published under the title
Steps to Christ.

Cover Credits:
K. Vreeland / H. Armstrong Roberts
Cover layout and design by C. E. Wheeling

ISBN: 0-916547-12-4
Printed in U.S.A.

Contents
PART I

THE WAY TO CHRIST

Contents
PART II

The Christian Way

PART I

THE WAY TO CHRIST

"Jesus saith unto him, I am the way, the truth, and the life: no man cometh unto the Father, but by me." John 14:6

PART I

THE WAY
TO CHRIST

"Jesus saith unto him, I am the way,
the truth, and the life: no man cometh
unto the Father, but by me." John XIV:6.

CHAPTER 1

THE SOURCE OF PEACE

NATURE AND REVELATION alike testify of God's love. Our Father in heaven is the source of life, of wisdom, and of joy. Look at the wonderful and beautiful things of nature. Think of their marvelous adaptation to the needs and happiness, not only of man, but of all living creatures. The sunshine and the rain, that gladden and refresh the earth, the hills and seas and plains, all speak to us of the Creator's love. It is God who supplies the daily needs of all His creatures. In the beautiful words of the psalmist,

> "The eyes of all wait upon Thee;
> And Thou givest them their meat in due season.
> Thou openest Thine hand,
> And satisfiest the desire of every living thing."
> Psalm 145:15, 16.

God made man perfectly holy and happy; and the fair earth, as it came from the Creator's hand, bore no blight of decay or shadow of the curse. It is transgression of God's law—the law of love—that has brought woe and death. Yet even amid the suffering that results from sin, God's love is revealed. It is written that God cursed the ground for man's sake. Genesis 3:17. The thorn and the thistle—the difficulties and trials that make his life one of toil and care—were appointed for his good, as a part of the training needful in God's plan for his uplifting from the ruin and degradation that sin has wrought. The world, though fallen, is not all sorrow and misery. In nature itself are messages of hope and comfort. There are flowers upon the thistles, and the thorns are covered with roses.

"God is love," is written upon every opening bud, upon every spire of springing grass. The lovely birds making the air vocal with their happy songs, the delicately tinted flowers in their perfection perfuming the air, the lofty trees of the forest with their rich foliage of living green—all testify to the tender, fatherly care of our God, and to His desire to make His children happy.

The Word of God reveals His character. He Himself has declared His infinite love and pity. When Moses prayed, "Show me Thy glory," the Lord answered, "I will make all My goodness pass before thee." Exodus 33:18, 19. This is His glory. The Lord passed before Moses, and proclaimed, "The Lord, The Lord God, merciful and gracious, long-suffering, and abundant in goodness and truth, keeping mercy for thousands, forgiving iniquity and transgression and sin." Exodus 34:6, 7. He is "slow to anger, and of great kindness," (Jonah 4:2), "because He delighteth in mercy." Micah 7:18.

God has bound our hearts to Him by unnumbered tokens in heaven and in earth. Through the things of nature, and the deepest and tenderest earthly ties that human hearts can know, He has sought to reveal Himself to us. Yet these but imperfectly represent His love. Though all these evidences have been given, the enemy of good blinded the minds of men, so that they looked upon God with fear; they thought of Him as severe and unforgiving. Satan led men to conceive of God as a being whose chief attribute is stern justice—one who is a severe judge, a harsh, exacting creditor. He pictured the Creator as a being who is watching with jealous eye to discern the errors and mistakes of men, that He may visit judgments upon them. It was to remove this dark shadow, by revealing to the world the infinite love of God, that Jesus came to live among men.

The Son of God came from heaven to make manifest the Father. "No man hath seen God at any time; the only begotten Son, which is in the bosom of the Father, He hath declared Him." John 1:18. "Neither knoweth any man the Father, save the Son, and he to whomsoever the

Son will reveal Him." Matthew 11:27. When one of the disciples made the request, "Show us the Father," Jesus answered, "Have I been so long time with you, and yet hast thou not known Me, Philip? He that hath seen Me hath seen the Father; and how sayest thou then, Show us the Father?" John 14:8, 9.

In describing His earthly mission, Jesus said, The Lord "hath anointed Me to preach the gospel to the poor; He hath sent Me to heal the brokenhearted, to preach deliverance to the captives, and recovering of sight to the blind, to set at liberty them that are bruised." Luke 4:18. This was His work. He went about doing good, and healing all that were oppressed by Satan. There were whole villages where there was not a moan of sickness in any house; for He had passed through them, and healed all their sick. His work gave evidence of His divine anointing. Love, mercy, and compassion were revealed in every act of His life; His heart went out in tender sympathy to the children of men. He took man's nature, that He might reach man's wants. The poorest and humblest were not afraid to approach Him. Even little children were attracted to Him. They loved to climb upon His knees, and gaze into the pensive face, benignant with love.

Jesus did not suppress one word of truth, but He uttered it always in love. He exercised the greatest tact, and thoughtful, kind attention, in His communion with the people. He was never rude, never needlessly spoke a severe word, never gave needless pain to a sensitive soul. He did not censure human weakness. He spoke the truth, but always in love. He denounced hypocrisy, unbelief, and iniquity; but tears were in His voice as He uttered His scathing rebukes. He wept over Jerusalem, the city He loved, which refused to receive Him, the Way, the Truth, and the Life. They had rejected Him, the Saviour, but He regarded them with pitying tenderness. His life was one of self-denial and thoughtful care for others. Every soul was precious in His eyes. While He ever bore Himself with divine dignity, He bowed with the tenderest regard to

every member of the family of God. In all men He saw
fallen souls whom it was His mission to save.

Such is the character of Christ as revealed in His life.
This is the character of God. It is from the Father's heart
that the streams of divine compassion, manifest in Christ,
flow out to the children of men. Jesus, the tender, pitying
Saviour, was God "manifest in the flesh." 1 Timothy
3:16.

It was to redeem us that Jesus lived and suffered and
died. He became a "Man of Sorrows," that we might be
made partakers of everlasting joy. God permitted His
beloved Son, full of grace and truth, to come from a world
of indescribable glory, to a world marred and blighted with
sin, darkened with the shadow of death and the curse. He
permitted Him to leave the bosom of His love, the
adoration of the angels, to suffer shame, insult,
humiliation, hatred, and death. "The chastisement of our
peace was upon Him; and with His stripes we are healed."
Isaiah 53:5. Behold Him in the wilderness, in
Gethsemane, upon the cross! The spotless Son of God
took upon Himself the burden of sin. He who had been
one with God, felt in His soul the awful separation that
sin makes between God and man. This wrung from His
lips the anguished cry, "My God, My God, why hast
Thou forsaken Me?" Matthew 27:46. It was the burden
of sin, the sense of its terrible enormity, of its separation
of the soul from God—it was this that broke the heart of
the Son of God.

But this great sacrifice was not made in order to create
in the Father's heart a love for man, not to make Him
willing to save. No, no! "God so loved the world, that
He gave His only begotten Son." John 3:16. The Father
loves us, not because of the great propitiation, but He
provided the propitiation because He loves us. Christ was
the medium through which He could pour out His infinite
love upon a fallen world. "God was in Christ, reconciling
the world unto Himself." 2 Corinthians 5:19. God
suffered with His Son. In the agony of Gethsemane, the
death of Calvary, the heart of Infinite Love paid the price

of our redemption.

Jesus said, "Therefore doth My Father love Me, because I lay down My life, that I might take it again." John 10:17. That is, "My Father has so loved you that He even loves Me more for giving My life to redeem you. In becoming your Substitute and Surety, by surrendering My life, by taking your liabilities, your transgressions, I am endeared to My Father; for by My Sacrifice, God can be just, and yet the Justifier of him who believeth in Jesus."

None but the Son of God could accomplish our redemption; for only He who was in the bosom of the Father could declare Him. Only He who knew the height and depth of the love of God could make it manifest. Nothing less than the infinite sacrifice made by Christ in behalf of fallen man could express the Father's love to lost humanity.

"God so loved the world, that He gave His only begotten Son." He gave Him not only to live among men, to bear their sins, and die their sacrifice. He gave Him to the fallen race. Christ was to identify Himself with the interests and needs of humanity. He who was one with God has linked Himself with the children of men by ties that are never to be broken. Jesus is "not ashamed to call them brethren" (Hebrews 2:11); He is our Sacrifice, our Advocate, our Brother, bearing our human form before the Father's throne, and through eternal ages one with the race He has redeemed—the Son of man. And all this that man might be uplifted from the ruin and degradation of sin that he might reflect the love of God, and share the joy of holiness.

The price paid for our redemption, the infinite sacrifice of our heavenly Father in giving His Son to die for us, should give us exalted conceptions of what we may become through Christ. As the inspired apostle John beheld the height, the depth, the breadth of the Father's love toward the perishing race, he was filled with adoration and reverence; and, failing to find suitable language in which to express the greatness and tenderness of this love, he called upon the world to behold it. "Behold, what manner of love the Father hath bestowed upon us, that we should be called the sons of God." 1 John 3:1. What a value this places upon man! Through transgression, the sons of man become subjects of Satan. Through faith in the atoning sacrifice of Christ, the sons of Adam may become the sons of God. By assuming human nature, Christ elevates humanity. Fallen men are placed where, through connection with Christ, they may indeed become worthy of the name "sons of God."

Such love is without a parallel. Children of the heavenly King! Precious promise! Theme for the most profound meditation! The matchless love of God for a world that did not love Him! The thought has a subduing power upon the soul, and brings the mind into captivity to the will of God. The more we study the divine character in the light of the cross, the more we see mercy, tenderness, and forgiveness blended with equity and justice, and the more clearly we discern innumerable evidences of a love that is infinite, and a tender pity surpassing a mother's yearning sympathy for her wayward child.

CHAPTER 2

YOUR NEED FOR PEACE

MAN WAS ORIGINALLY endowed with noble powers and a well-balanced mind. He was perfect in his being, and in harmony with God. His thoughts were pure, his aims holy. But through disobedience, his powers were perverted, and selfishness took the place of love. His nature became so weakened through transgression that it was impossible for him, in his own strength, to resist the power of evil. He was made captive by Satan, and would have remained so forever had not God specially interposed. It was the tempter's purpose to thwart the divine plan in man's creation, and fill the earth with woe and desolation. And he would point to all this evil as the result of God's work in creating man.

In his sinless state, man held joyful communion with Him "in whom are hid all the treasures of wisdom and knowledge." Colossians 2:3. But after his sin, he could no longer find joy in holiness, and he sought to hide from the presence of God. Such is still the condition of the unrenewed heart. It is not in harmony with God, and finds no joy in communion with Him. The sinner could not be happy in God's presence; he would shrink from the companionship of holy beings. Could he be permitted to enter heaven, it would have no joy for him. The spirit of unselfish love that reigns there—every heart responding to the heart of Infinite Love—would touch no answering chord in his soul. His thoughts, his interests, his motives, would be alien to those that actuate the sinless dwellers there. He would be a discordant note in the melody of heaven. Heaven would be to him a place of torture; he would long to be hidden from Him who is its light, and the center of its joy. It is no arbitrary decree on the part of God that excludes the wicked from heaven: they are shut out by their own unfitness for its companionship. The glory of God would be to them a consuming fire. They would welcome destruction, that they might be hidden from the face of Him who died to redeem them.

It is impossible for us, of ourselves, to escape from the pit of sin in which we are sunken. Our hearts are evil, and we cannot change them. "Who can bring a clean thing out of an unclean? not one." "The carnal mind is enmity against God: for it is not subject to the law of God, neither indeed can be." Job 14:4; Romans 8:7. Education, culture, the exercise of the will, human effort, all have their proper sphere, but here they are powerless. They may produce an outward correctness of behavior, but they cannot change the heart; they cannot purify the springs of life. There must be a power working from within, a new life from above, before men can be changed from sin to holiness. That power is Christ. His grace alone can quicken the lifeless faculties of the soul, and attract it to God, to holiness.

The Saviour said, "Except a man be born from above," unless he shall receive a new heart, new desires, purposes, and motives, leading to a new life, "he cannot see the kingdom of God." John 3:3, margin. The idea that it is necessary only to develop the good that exists in man by nature, is a fatal deception. "The natural man receiveth not the things of the Spirit of God: for they are foolishness unto him; neither can he know them, because they are spiritually discerned." "Marvel not that I said unto thee, Ye must be born again." 1 Corinthians 2:14; John 3:7. Of Christ it is written, "In Him was life; and the life was the light of men"—the only "name under heaven given among men, whereby we must be saved." John 1:4; Acts 4:12.

It is not enough to perceive the loving-kindness of God, to see the benevolence, the fatherly tenderness, of His character. It is not enough to discern the wisdom and justice of His law, to see that it is founded upon the eternal principle of love. Paul the apostle saw all this when he exclaimed, "I consent unto the law that it is good." "The law is holy, and the commandment holy, and just, and good." But he added, in the bitterness of his soul-anguish and despair, "I am carnal, sold under sin." Romans 7:16, 12, 14. He longed for the purity, the righteousness, to which in himself he was powerless to attain, and he cried out, "O wretched man that I am! who shall deliver me from this body of death?" Romans 7:24, margin. Such is the cry that has gone up from burdened hearts in all lands and in all ages. To all, there is but one answer, "Behold the Lamb of God, which taketh away the sin of the world." John 1:29.

Many are the figures by which the Spirit of God has sought to illustrate this truth, and make it plain to souls that long to be freed from the burden of guilt. When, after his sin in deceiving Esau, Jacob fled from his father's home, he was weighed down with a sense of guilt. Lonely and outcast as he was, separated from all that had made life dear, the one thought that above all others pressed upon his soul, was the fear that his sin had cut him off from God, that he was forsaken of Heaven. In sadness he lay down to rest on the bare earth, around him only the lonely hills, and above, the heavens bright with stars. As he slept, a strange light broke upon his vision; and lo, from the plain on which he lay, vast shadowy stairs seemed to lead upward to the very gates of heaven, and upon them angels of God were passing up and down; while from the glory above, the divine voice was heard in a message of comfort and hope. Thus was made known to Jacob that which met the need and longing of his soul—a Saviour. With joy and gratitude he saw revealed a way by which he, a sinner, could be restored to communion with God. The mystic ladder of his dream represented Jesus, the only medium of communication between God and man.

This is the same figure to which Christ referred in his conversation with Nathanael, when He said, "Ye shall see heaven open, and the angels of God ascending and descending upon the Son of man." John 1:51. In the apostasy, man alienated himself from God; earth was cut off from heaven. Across the gulf that lay between, there could be no communion. But through Christ, earth is again linked with heaven. With His own merits, Christ has bridged the gulf which sin had made, so that the ministering angels can hold communion with man. Christ connects fallen man in his weakness and helplessness with the Source of infinite power.

But in vain are men's dreams of progress, in vain all efforts for the uplifting of humanity, if they neglect the one Source of hope and help for the fallen race. "Every good gift and every perfect gift" (James 1:17), is from God. There is no true excellence of character apart from Him. And the only way to God is Christ. He says, "I am the way, the truth and the life: no man cometh unto the Father, but by Me." John 14:6.

The heart of God yearns over His earthly children with a love stronger than death. In giving up His Son, He has poured out to us all heaven in one gift. The Saviour's life and death and intercession, the ministry of angels, the pleading of the Spirit, the Father working above and through all, the unceasing interest of heavenly beings—all are enlisted in behalf of man's redemption.

O let us contemplate the amazing sacrifice that has been made for us! Let us try to appreciate the labor and energy that Heaven is expending to reclaim the lost, and bring them back to the Father's house. Motives stronger, and agencies more powerful, could never be brought into operation; the exceeding rewards for right-doing, the enjoyment of heaven, the society of the angels, the communion and love of God and His Son, the elevation and extension of all our powers throughout eternal ages— are these not mighty incentives and encouragements to urge us to give the heart's loving service to our Creator and Redeemer?

And, on the other hand, the judgments of God pronounced against sin, the inevitable retribution, the degradation of our character, and the final destruction are presented in God's Word to warn us against the service of

Satan.

Shall we not regard the mercy of God? What more could He do? Let us place ourselves in right relation to Him who has loved us with amazing love. Let us avail ourselves of the means provided for us that we may be transformed into His likeness, and be restored to fellowship with the ministering angels, to harmony and communion with the Father and the Son.

CHAPTER 3

THE GUILT FACTOR

HOW SHALL A MAN be just with God? How shall the sinner be made righteous? It is only through Christ that we can be brought into harmony with God, with holiness; but how are we to come to Christ? Many are asking the same question as did the multitude on the Day of Pentecost, when, convicted of sin, they cried out, "What shall we do?" The first word of Peter's answer was, "Repent." Acts 2:38. At another time, shortly after, he said, "Repent, . . . and be converted, that your sins may be blotted out." Acts 3:19.

Repentance includes sorrow for sin, and a turning away from it. We shall not renounce sin unless we see its sinfulness; until we turn away from it in heart, there will be no real change in the life.

There are many who fail to understand the true nature of repentance. Multitudes sorrow that they have sinned, and even make an outward reformation, because they fear that their wrongdoing will bring suffering upon themselves. But this is not repentance in the Bible sense. They lament the suffering, rather than the sin. Such was the grief of Esau when he saw that the birthright was lost to him forever. Balaam, terrified by the angel standing in his pathway with drawn sword, acknowledged his guilt lest he should lose his life; but there was no genuine repentance for sin, no conversion of purpose, no abhorrence of evil. Judas Iscariot, after betraying his Lord, exclaimed, "I have sinned in that I have betrayed the innocent blood." Matthew 27:4.

The confession was forced from his guilty soul by an awful sense of condemnation and a fearful looking for of judgment. The consequences that were to result to him filled him with terror, but there was no deep, heartbreaking grief in his soul, that he had betrayed the spotless Son of God, and denied the Holy One of Israel. Pharaoh, when suffering under the judgments of God, acknowledged his sin in order to escape further punishment, but returned to his defiance of Heaven as soon as the plagues were stayed. These all lamented the results of sin, but did not sorrow for the sin itself.

But when the heart yields to the influence of the Spirit of God, the conscience will be quickened, and the sinner will discern something of the depth and sacredness of God's holy law, the foundation of His government in heaven and on earth. The "Light which lighteth every man that cometh into the world" (John 1:9), illumines the secret chambers of the soul, and the hidden things of darkness are made manifest. Conviction takes hold upon the mind and heart. The sinner has a sense of the righteousness of Jehovah, and feels the terror of appearing, in his own guilt and uncleanness, before the Searcher of hearts. He sees the love of God, the beauty of holiness, the joy of purity; he longs to be cleansed, and to be restored to communion with Heaven.

The prayer of David after his fall, illustrates the nature of true sorrow for sin. His repentance was sincere and deep. There was no effort to palliate his guilt; no desire to escape the judgment threatened, inspired his prayer. David saw the enormity of his transgression; he saw the defilement of his soul; he loathed his sin. It was not for pardon only that he prayed, but for purity of heart. He longed for the joy of holiness—to be restored to harmony and communion with God. This was the language of his soul:

> "Blessed is he whose transgression is forgiven, whose sin is covered.
> Blessed is the man unto whom the Lord imputeth not iniquity,
> And in whose spirit there is no guile."

> Psalm 32:1, 2.

"Have mercy upon me, O God, according to Thy
lovingkindness:
According unto the multitude of Thy tender mercies
blot out my transgressions...
For I acknowledge my transgressions: and my sin is
ever before me...
Purge me with hyssop, and I shall be clean: wash me,
and I shall be whiter than snow...

Create in me a clean heart, O God;
And renew a right spirit within me.
Cast me not away from Thy presence;
And take not Thy Holy Spirit from me.
Restore unto me the joy of Thy salvation;
And uphold me with Thy free spirit...
Deliver me from bloodguiltiness, O God, Thou God
of my salvation!
And my tongue shall sing aloud of Thy
righteousness."

                                        Psalm 51:1-14.

A repentance such as this, is beyond the reach of our
own power to accomplish; it is obtained only from
Christ, who ascended up on high, and has given gifts unto
men.

Just here is a point on which many may err, and
hence they fail of receiving the help that Christ desires to
give them. They think that they cannot come to Christ
unless they first repent, and that repentance prepares for
the forgiveness of their sins. It is true that repentance
does precede the forgiveness of sins; for it is only the
broken and contrite heart that will feel the need of a
Saviour. But must the sinner wait till he has repented
before he can come to Jesus? Is repentance to be made an
obstacle between the sinner and the Saviour?

The Bible does not teach that the sinner must repent
before he can heed the invitation of Christ, "Come unto
Me, all ye that labor and are heavy laden, and I will give

you rest." Matthew 11:28. It is the virtue that goes forth from Christ, that leads to genuine repentance. Peter made the matter clear in his statement to the Israelites, when he said, "Him hath God exalted with His right hand to be a Prince and a Saviour, for to give repentance to Israel, and forgiveness of sins." Acts 5:31. We can no more repent without the Spirit of Christ to awaken the conscience than we can be pardoned without Christ.

Christ is the source of every right impulse. He is the only one that can implant in the heart enmity against sin. Every desire for truth and purity, every conviction of our own sinfulness, is an evidence that His Spirit is moving upon our hearts.

Jesus has said, "I, if I be lifted up from the earth, will draw all men unto me." John 12:32. Christ must be revealed to the sinner as the Saviour dying for the sins of the world; and as we behold the Lamb of God upon the cross of Calvary, the mystery of redemption begins to unfold to our minds, and the goodness of God leads us to repentance. In dying for sinners, Christ manifested a love that is incomprehensible; and as the sinner beholds this love, it softens the heart, impresses the mind, and inspires contrition in the soul.

It is true that men sometimes become ashamed of their sinful ways, and give up some of their evil habits, before they are conscious that they are being drawn to Christ. But whenever they make an effort to reform, from a sincere desire to do right, it is the power of Christ that is drawing them. An influence of which they are unconscious works upon the soul, and the conscience is quickened, and the outward life is amended. And as Christ draws them to look upon His cross, to behold Him whom their sins have pierced, the commandment comes home to the conscience. The wickedness of their life, the deep-seated sin of the soul, is revealed to them. They begin to comprehend something of the righteousness of Christ, and exclaim, "What is sin, that it should require such a sacrifice for the redemption of its victim? Was all this love, all this suffering, all this humiliation demanded, that we might not perish, but have everlasting life?"

The sinner may resist this love, may refuse to be drawn to Christ; but if he does not resist, he will be drawn to Jesus; a knowledge of the plan of salvation will lead him to the foot of the cross in repentance for his sins, which have caused the sufferings of God's dear Son.

The same divine mind that is working upon the things of nature is speaking to the hearts of men, and creating an inexpressible craving for something they have not. The things of the world cannot satisfy their longing. The Spirit of God is pleading with them to seek for those things that alone can give peace and rest—the grace of Christ, the joy of holiness. Through influences seen and unseen, our Saviour is constantly at work to attract the minds of men from the unsatisfying pleasures of sin to the infinite blessings that may be theirs in Him. To all these souls, who are vainly seeking to drink from the broken cisterns of this world, the divine message is addressed, "Let him that is athirst come. And whosoever will, let him take the water of life freely." Revelation 22:17.

You who in heart long for something better than this world can give, recognize this longing as the voice of God to your soul. Ask Him to give you repentance, to reveal Christ to you in His infinite love, in His perfect purity. In the Saviour's life the principles of God's law—love to God and man—were perfectly exemplified. Benevolence, unselfish love, was the life of His soul. It is as we behold Him, as the light from our Saviour falls upon us, that we see the sinfulness of our own hearts.

We may have flattered ourselves, as did Nicodemus, that our life has been upright, that our moral character is correct, and think that we need not humble the heart before God, like the common sinner: but when the light from Christ shines into our souls, we shall see how impure we are; we shall discern the selfishness of motive, the enmity against God, that has defiled every act of life. Then we shall know that our own righteousness is indeed as filthy rags, and that the blood of Christ alone can cleanse us from the defilement of sin, and renew our hearts in His own likeness.

One ray of the glory of God, one gleam of the purity of Christ, penetrating the soul, makes every spot of defilement painfully distinct, and lays bare the deformity and defects of the human character. It makes apparent the unhallowed desires, the infidelity of the heart, the impurity of the lips. The sinner's acts of disloyalty in making void the law of God, are exposed to his sight, and his spirit is stricken and afflicted under the searching influence of the Spirit of God. He loathes himself as he views the pure, spotless character of Christ.

When the prophet Daniel beheld the glory surrounding the heavenly messenger that was sent unto him, he was overwhelmed with a sense of his own weakness and imperfection. Describing the effect of the wonderful scene, he says, "There remained no strength in me: for my comeliness was turned in me into corruption, and I retained no strength." Daniel 10:8. The soul thus touched will hate its selfishness, abhor its self-love, and will seek, through Christ's righteousness, for the purity of heart that is in harmony with the law of God and the character of Christ.

Paul says that as "touching the righteousness which is in the law"—as far as outward acts were concerned—he was "blameless" (Philippians 3:6); but when the spiritual character of the law was discerned, he saw himself a sinner. Judged by the letter of the law as men apply it to the outward life, he had abstained from sin; but when he looked into the depths of its holy precepts, and saw himself as God saw him, he bowed in humiliation, and confessed his guilt. He says, "I was alive without the law once: but when the commandment came, sin revived, and I died." Romans 7:9. When he saw the spiritual nature of the law, sin appeared in its true hideousness, and his self-esteem was gone.

God does not regard all sin as of equal magnitude; there are degrees of guilt in His estimation, as well as in that of man; but however trifling this or that wrong act may seem in the eyes of men, no sin is small in the sight of God. Man's judgment is partial, imperfect; but God estimates all things as they really are. The drunkard is despised, and is told that his sin will exclude him from heaven; while pride, selfishness, and covetousness too often go unrebuked. But these are sins that are especially offensive to God; for they are contrary to the benevolence of His character, to that unselfish love which is the very atmosphere of the unfallen universe. He who falls into some of the grosser sins may feel a sense of his shame and poverty and his need of the grace of Christ; but pride feels no need, and so it closes the heart against Christ, and the infinite blessings He came to give.

The poor publican who prayed, "God be merciful to me a sinner" (Luke 18:13), regarded himself as a very wicked man, and others looked upon him in the same light; but he felt his need, and with his burden of guilt and shame he came before God, asking for His mercy. His heart was open for the Spirit of God to do its gracious work, and set him free from the power of sin. The Pharisee's boastful, self-righteous prayer showed that his heart was closed against the influence of the Holy Spirit. Because of his distance from God, he had no sense of his own defilement, in contrast with the perfection of the divine holiness. He felt no need, and he received nothing.

If you see your sinfulness, do not wait to make yourself better. How many there are who think they are not good enough to come to Christ. Do you expect to become better through your own efforts? "Can the Ethiopian change his skin, or the leopard his spots? then may ye also do good, that are accustomed to do evil." Jeremiah 13:23. There is help for us only in God. We must not wait for stronger persuasions, for better opportunities, or for holier tempers. We can do nothing of ourselves. We must come to Christ just as we are.

But let none deceive themselves with the thought that God, in His great love and mercy, will yet save even the rejectors of His grace. The exceeding sinfulness of sin can be estimated only in the light of the cross. When men urge that God is too good to cast off the sinner, let them look to Calvary. It was because there was no other way in which man could be saved, because without this sacrifice it was impossible for the human race to escape from the defiling power of sin, and be restored to communion with holy beings—impossible for them again to become partakers of spiritual life—it was because of this that Christ took upon Himself the guilt of the disobedient, and suffered in the sinner's stead. The love and suffering and death of the Son of God all testify to the terrible enormity of sin, and declare that there is no escape from its power, no hope of the higher life, but through the submission of the soul to Christ.

The impenitent sometimes excuse themselves by saying of professed Christians, "I am as good as they are. They are no more self-denying, sober, or circumspect in their conduct that I am. They love pleasure and self-indulgence as well as I do." Thus they make the faults of others an excuse for their own neglect of duty. But the sins and defects of others do not excuse anyone; for the Lord has not given us an erring human pattern. The spotless Son of God has been given as our example, and those who complain of the wrong course of professed Christians are the ones who should show better lives and nobler examples. If they have so high a conception of what a Christian should be, is not their own sin so much the greater? They know what is right, and yet refuse to do it.

Beware of procrastination. Do not put off the work of forsaking your sins, and seeking purity of heart through Jesus. Here is where thousands upon thousands have erred, to their eternal loss. I will not here dwell upon the shortness and uncertainty of life; but there is a terrible danger—a danger not sufficiently understood—in delaying to yield to the pleading voice of God's Holy Spirit, in choosing to live in sin; for such this delay really is. Sin, however small it may be esteemed, can be indulged in only at the peril of infinite loss. What we do not overcome, will overcome us, and work out our destruction.

Adam and Eve persuaded themselves that in so small a matter as eating of the forbidden fruit, there could not result such terrible consequences as God had declared. But this small matter was the transgression of God's immutable and holy law, and it separated man from God, and opened the floodgates of death and untold woe upon our world. Age after age there has gone up from our earth a continual cry of mourning, and the whole creation groaneth and travaileth together in pain, as a consequence of man's disobedience. Heaven itself has felt the effects of his rebellion against God. Calvary stands as a memorial of the amazing sacrifice required to atone for the transgression of the divine law. Let us not regard sin as a trivial thing.

Every act of transgression, every neglect or rejection of the grace of Christ, is reacting upon yourself; it is hardening the heart, depraving the will, benumbing the understanding, and not only making you less inclined to yield, but less capable of yielding, to the tender pleading of God's Holy Spirit.

Many are quieting a troubled conscience with the thought that they can change a course of evil when they choose; that they can trifle with the invitations of mercy, and yet be again and again impressed. They think that after doing despite to the Spirit of grace, after casting their influence on the side of Satan, in a moment of terrible extremity they can change their course. But this is not so easily done. The experience, the education, of a lifetime, has so thoroughly molded the character that few then desire to receive the image of Jesus.

Even one wrong trait of character, one sinful desire, persistently cherished, will eventually neutralize all the power of the gospel. Every sinful indulgence strengthens the soul's aversion to God. The man who manifests an infidel hardihood, or a stolid indifference to divine truth, is but reaping the harvest of that which he has himself sown. In all the Bible there is not a more fearful warning against trifling with evil than the words of the wise man, that the sinner "shall be holden with the cords of his sins." Proverbs 5:22.

Christ is ready to set us free from sin, but He does not force the will; and if by persistent transgression the will itself is wholly bent on evil, and we do not *desire* to be set free, if we *will* not accept His grace, what more can He do? We have destroyed ourselves by our determined rejection of His love. "Behold, now is the accepted time; behold, now is the day of salvation." "Today if ye will hear His voice, harden not your hearts." 2 Corinthians 6:2; Hebrews 3:7, 8.

"Man looketh on the outward appearance, but the Lord looketh on the heart"—the human heart, with its conflicting emotions of joy and sorrow; the wandering, wayward heart, which is the abode of so much impurity and deceit. 1 Samuel 16:7. He knows its motives, its very intents and purposes. Go to Him with your soul all stained as it is. Like the psalmist, throw its chambers open to the all-seeing eye, exclaiming, "Search me, O God, and know my heart: try me, and know my thoughts: and see if there be any wicked way in me, and lead me in the way everlasting." Psalm 139:23, 24.

Many accept an intellectual religion, a form of godliness, when the heart is not cleansed. Let it be your prayer, "Create in me a clean heart, O God; and renew a right spirit within me." Psalm 51:10. Deal truly with your own soul. Be as earnest, as persistent, as you would be if your mortal life were at stake. This is a matter to be settled between God and your own soul, settled for eternity. A supposed hope, and nothing more, will prove your ruin.

Study God's Word prayerfully. That Word presents before you, in the law of God and the life of Christ, the great principles of holiness, without which "no man shall see the Lord." Hebrews 12:14. It convinces of sin; it plainly reveals the way of salvation. Give heed to it, as the voice of God speaking to your soul.

As you see the enormity of sin, as you see yourself as you really are, do not give up to despair. It was sinners that Christ came to save. We have not to reconcile God to us, but—O wondrous love!—God in Christ is "reconciling the world unto Himself." 2 Corinthians 5:19. He is wooing by His tender love the hearts of His erring children. No earthly parent could be as patient with the faults and mistakes of his children, as is God with those He seeks to save. No one could plead more tenderly with the transgressor. No human lips ever poured out more tender entreaties to the wanderer than does He. All His promises, His warnings, are but the breathing of unutterable love.

When Satan comes to tell you that you are a great sinner, look up to your Redeemer, and talk of His merits. That which will help you is to look to His light. Acknowledge your sin, but tell the enemy that "Christ Jesus came into the world to save sinners," (1 Timothy 1:15), and that you may be saved by His matchless love. Jesus asked Simon a question in regard to two debtors. One owed his lord a small sum, and the other owed him a very large sum; but he forgave them both, and Christ asked Simon which debtor would love his lord most. Simon answered, "He to whom he forgave most." Luke 7:43. We have been great sinners, but Christ died that we might be forgiven. The merits of His sacrifice are sufficient to present to the Father in our behalf. Those to whom He has forgiven most will love Him most, and will stand nearest to His throne to praise Him for His great love and infinite sacrifice. It is when we most fully comprehend the love of God that we best realize the sinfulness of sin. When we see the length of the chain that was let down for us, when we understand something of the infinite sacrifice that Christ has made in our behalf, the heart is melted with tenderness and contrition.

CHAPTER 4

LIVING WITH YOUR CONSCIENCE

"HE THAT COVERETH his sins shall not prosper: but whoso confesseth and forsaketh them shall have mercy." Proverbs 28:13.

The conditions of obtaining mercy of God are simple and just and reasonable. The Lord does not require us to do some grievous thing in order that we may have the forgiveness of sin. We need not make long and wearisome pilgrimages, or perform painful penances, to commend our souls to the God of heaven or to expiate our transgression; but he that confesseth and forsaketh his sin shall have mercy.

The apostle says, "Confess your faults one to another, and pray one for another, that ye may be healed." James 5:16. Confess your sins to God, who only can forgive them, and your faults to one another. If you have given offense to your friend or neighbor, you are to acknowledge your wrong, and it is his duty freely to forgive you. Then you are to seek the forgiveness of God, because the brother you have wounded is the property of God, and in injuring him you sinned against his Creator and Redeemer. The case is brought before the only true Mediator, our great High Priest, who "was in all points tempted like as we are, yet without sin," and who is "touched with the feeling of our infirmities" (Hebrews 4:15), and is able to cleanse from every stain of iniquity.

Those who have not humbled their souls before God in acknowledging their guilt, have not yet fulfilled the first condition of acceptance. If we have not experienced that repentance which is not to be repented of, and have not with true humiliation of soul and brokenness of spirit confessed our sins, abhorring our iniquity, we have never

31

truly sought for the forgiveness of sin; and if we have never sought, we have never found the peace of God. The only reason why we do not have remission of sins that are past is that we are not willing to humble our hearts and comply with the conditions of the word of truth. Explicit instruction is given concerning this matter. Confession of sin, whether public or private, should be heartfelt, and freely expressed. It is not to be urged from the sinner. It is not to be made in a flippant and careless way, or forced from those who have no realizing sense of the abhorrent character of sin. The confession that is the outpouring of the inmost soul finds its way to the God of infinite pity. The psalmist says, "The Lord is nigh unto them that are of a broken heart; and saveth such as be of a contrite spirit." Psalm 34:18.

True confession is always of a specific character, and acknowledges particular sins. They may be of such a nature as to be brought before God only; they may be wrongs that should be confessed to individuals who have suffered injury through them; or they may be of a public character, and should then be as publicly confessed. But all confession should be definite and to the point, acknowledging the very sins of which you are guilty.

In the days of Samuel, the Israelites wandered from God. They were suffering the consequences of sin; for they had lost their faith in God, lost their discernment of His power and wisdom to rule the nation, lost their confidence in His ability to defend and vindicate His cause. They turned from the great Ruler of the universe, and desired to be governed as were the nations around them. Before they found peace, they made this definite confession: "We have added unto all our sins this evil, to ask us a king." 1 Samuel 12:19. The very sin of which they were convicted had to be confessed. Their ingratitude oppressed their souls, and severed them from God.

Confession will not be acceptable to God without sincere repentance and reformation. There must be decided changes in the life; everything offensive to God must be put away. This will be the result of genuine sorrow for sin. The work that we have to do on our part is plainly set before us: "Wash you, make you clean; put away the evil of your doings from before Mine eyes; cease to do evil; learn to do well; seek judgment, relieve the oppressed, judge the fatherless, plead for the widow." Isaiah 1:16, 17. "If the wicked restore the pledge, give again that he had robbed, walk in the statutes of life, without committing iniquity; he shall surely live, he shall not die." Ezekiel 33:15. Paul says, speaking of the work of repentance: "Ye sorrowed after a godly sort, what carefulness it wrought in you, yea, what clearing of yourselves, yea, what indignation, yea, what fear, yea, what vehement desire, yea, what zeal, yea, what revenge! In all things ye have approved yourselves to be clear in this matter." 2 Corinthians 7:11.

When sin has deadened the moral perceptions, the wrongdoer does not discern the defects of his character, nor realize the enormity of the evil he has committed; and unless he yields to the convicting power of the Holy Spirit, he remains in partial blindness to his sin. His confessions are not sincere and in earnest. To every acknowledgement of his guilt he adds an apology in excuse of his course, declaring that if it had not been for certain circumstances, he would not have done this or that, for which he is reproved.

After Adam and Eve had eaten of the forbidden fruit, they were filled with a sense of shame and terror. At first their only thought was how to excuse their sin, and escape the dreaded sentence of death. When the Lord inquired concerning their sin, Adam replied, laying the guilt partly upon God and partly upon his companion: "The woman whom Thou gavest to be with me, she gave me of the tree, and I did eat." The woman put the blame upon the serpent, saying, "The serpent beguiled me, and I did eat." Genesis 3:12, 13. Why did You make the serpent? Why did You suffer him to come into Eden? These were the questions implied in her excuse for her sin, thus charging God with the responsibility of their fall. The spirit of self-justification originated in the father of lies, and has been exhibited by all the sons and daughters of Adam. Confessions of this order are not inspired by the divine Spirit, and will not be acceptable to God. True repentance will lead a man to bear his guilt himself, and acknowledge it without deception or hypocrisy. Like the poor publican, not lifting up so much as his eyes unto heaven, he will cry, "God be merciful to me a sinner;" and those who do acknowledge their guilt will be justified; for Jesus will plead His blood in behalf of the repentant soul.

The examples in God's Word of genuine repentance and humiliation reveal a spirit of confession in which there is no excuse for sin, or attempt at self-justification. Paul did not seek to shield himself; he paints his sin in its darkest hue, not attempting to lessen his guilt. He says: "Many of the saints did I shut up in prison, having received authority from the chief priests; and when they were put to death, I gave my voice against them. And I punished them oft in every synagogue, and compelled them to blaspheme; and being exceedingly mad against them, I persecuted them even unto strange cities." Acts 26:10, 11. He does not hesitate to declare that "Christ Jesus came into the world to save sinners; of whom I am chief." 1 Timothy 1:15.

The humble and broken heart, subdued by genuine repentance, will appreciate something of the love of God and the cost of Calvary; and as a son confesses to a loving father, so will the truly penitent bring all his sins before God. And it is written, "If we confess our sins, He is faithful and just to forgive us our sins, and to cleanse us from all unrighteousness." 1 John 1:9.

CHAPTER 5

LIFE AT ITS BEST

GOD'S PROMISE IS, "Ye shall seek Me, and find Me, when ye shall search for Me with all your heart." Jeremiah 29:13.

The whole heart must be yielded to God, or the change can never be wrought in us by which we are to be restored to His likeness. By nature we are alienated from God. The Holy Spirit describes our condition in such words as these: "Dead in trespasses and sins;" "the whole head is sick, and the whole heart faint;" "no soundness in it." We are held fast in the snare of Satan; "taken captive by him at his will." Ephesians 2:1; Isaiah 1:5, 6; 2 Timothy 2:26. God desires to heal us, to set us free. But since this requires an entire transformation, a renewing of our whole nature, we must yield ourselves wholly to Him.

The warfare against self is the greatest battle that was ever fought. The yielding of self, surrendering all to the will of God, requires a struggle; but the soul must submit to God before it can be renewed in holiness.

The government of God is not, as Satan would make it appear, founded upon a blind submission, an unreasoning control. It appeals to the intellect and the conscience. "Come now, and let us reason together," (Isaiah 1:18), is the Creator's invitation to the beings He has made. God does not force the will of His creatures. He cannot accept an homage that is not willingly and intelligently given. A mere forced submission would prevent all real development of mind or character; it would make man a mere automaton. Such is not the purpose of the Creator. He desires that man, the crowning work of His creative power, shall reach the highest possible development. He sets before us the height of blessing to which He desires to bring us through His grace. He invites us to give ourselves to Him, that He may work His will in us. It remains for us to choose whether we will be set free from the bondage of sin, to share the glorious liberty of the sons of God.

In giving ourselves to God, we must necessarily give up all that would separate us from Him. Hence the Saviour says, "Whosoever he be of you that forsaketh not all that he hath, he cannot be My disciple." Luke 14:33. Whatever shall draw away the heart from God must be given up. Mammon is the idol of many. The love of money, the desire for wealth, is the golden chain that binds them to Satan. Reputation and worldly honor are worshiped by another class. The life of selfish ease and freedom from responsibility is the idol of others. But these slavish bands must be broken. We cannot be half the Lord's and half the world's. We are not God's children unless we are such entirely.

There are those who profess to serve God, while they rely upon their own efforts to obey His law, to form a right character, and secure salvation. Their hearts are not moved by any deep sense of the love of Christ, but they seek to perform the duties of the Christian life as that which God requires of them in order to gain heaven. Such religion is worth nothing. When Christ dwells in the heart, the soul will be so filled with His love, with the joy of communion with Him, that it will cleave to Him; and in the contemplation of Him, self will be forgotten. Love to Christ will be the spring of action. Those who feel the constraining love of God, do not ask how little may be given to meet the requirements of God; they do not ask for the lowest standard, but aim at perfect conformity to the will of their Redeemer. With earnest desire they yield all, and manifest an interest proportionate to the value of the object which they seek. A profession of Christ without this deep love, is mere talk, dry formality, and heavy drudgery.

Do you feel that it is too great a sacrifice to yield all

to Christ? Ask yourself the question, "What has Christ given for me?" The Son of God gave all—life and love and suffering—for our redemption. And can it be that we, the unworthy objects of so great love, will withhold our hearts from Him? Every moment of our lives we have been partakers of the blessings of His grace, and for this very reason we cannot fully realize the depths of ignorance and misery from which we have been saved. Can we look upon Him whom our sins have pierced, and yet be willing to do despite to all His love and sacrifice? In view of the infinite humiliation of the Lord of glory, shall we murmur because we can enter into life only through conflict and self-abasement?

The inquiry of many a proud heart is, "Why need I go in penitence and humiliation before I can have the assurance of my acceptance with God?" I point you to Christ. He was sinless, and, more than this, He was the Prince of heaven; but in man's behalf He became sin for the race. "He was numbered with the transgressors; and He bare the sin of many, and made intercession for the transgressors." Isaiah 53:12.

But what do we give up, when we give all? A sin-polluted heart, for Jesus to purify, to cleanse by His own blood, and to save by His matchless love. And yet men think it hard to give up all! I am ashamed to hear it spoken of, ashamed to write it.

God does not require us to give up anything that it is for our best interest to retain. In all that He does, He has the well-being of His children in view. Would that all who have not chosen Christ might realize that He has something vastly better to offer them than they are seeking for themselves. Man is doing the greatest injury and injustice to his own soul when he thinks and acts contrary to the will of God. No real joy can be found in the path forbidden by Him who knows what is best, and who plans for the good of His creatures. The path of transgression is the path of misery and destruction.

It is a mistake to entertain the thought that God is pleased to see His children suffer. All heaven is interested in the happiness of man. Our heavenly Father does not close the avenues of joy to any of His creatures. The divine requirements call upon us to shun those indulgences that would bring suffering and disappointment, that would close to us the door of happiness and heaven. The world's Redeemer accepts men as they are, with all their wants, imperfections, and weaknesses; and He will not only cleanse from sin and grant redemption through His blood, but will satisfy the heart-longing of all who consent to wear His yoke, to bear His burden. It is His purpose to impart peace and rest to all who come to Him for the bread of life. He requires us to perform only those duties that will lead our steps to heights of bliss to which the disobedient can never attain. The true, joyous life of the soul is to have Christ formed within, the hope of glory.

Many are inquiring, "*How* am I to make the surrender of myself to God?" You desire to give yourself to Him, but you are weak in moral power, in slavery to doubt, and controlled by the habits of your life of sin. Your promises and resolutions are like ropes of sand. You cannot control your thoughts, your impulses, your affections. The knowledge of your broken promises and forfeited pledges weakens your confidence in your own sincerity, and causes you to feel that God cannot accept you; but you need not despair. What you need to understand is the true force of the will. This is the governing power in the nature of man, the power of decision, or of choice. Everything depends on the right action of the will. The power of choice God has given to men; it is theirs to exercise. You cannot change your heart, you cannot of yourself give to God its affections; but you can *choose* to serve Him. You can give Him your will; He will then work in you to will and to do according to His good pleasure. Thus your whole nature will be brought under the control of the Spirit of Christ; your affections will be centered upon Him, your thoughts will be in harmony with Him.

Desires for goodness and holiness are right as far as

they go; but if you stop here, they will avail nothing. Many will be lost while hoping and desiring to be Christians. They do not come to the point of yielding the will to God. They do not now *choose* to be Christians.

Through the right exercise of the will, an entire change may be made in your life. By yielding up your will to Christ, you ally yourself with the power that is above all principalities and powers. You will have strength from above to hold you steadfast, and thus through constant surrender to God you will be enabled to live the new life, even the life of faith.

CHAPTER 6

THE ROLE OF FAITH

AS YOUR CONSCIENCE has been quickened by the Holy Spirit, you have seen something of the evil of sin, of its power, its guilt, its woe; and you look upon it with abhorrence. You feel that sin has separated you from God, that you are in bondage to the power of evil. The more you struggle to escape, the more you realize your helplessness. Your motives are impure; your heart is unclean. You see that your life has been filled with selfishness and sin. You long to be forgiven, to be cleansed, to be set free. Harmony with God, likeness to Him—what can you do to obtain it?

It is peace that you need—Heaven's forgiveness and peace and love in the soul. Money cannot buy it, intellect cannot procure it, wisdom cannot attain to it; you can never hope, by your own efforts, to secure it. But God offers it to you as a gift, "without money and without price." Isaiah 55:1. It is yours if you will but reach out your hand and grasp it. The Lord says, "Though your sins be as scarlet, they shall be as white as snow; though they be red like crimson, they shall be as wool." Isaiah 1:18. "A new heart also will I give you, and a new spirit will I put within you." Ezekiel 36:26.

You have confessed your sins, and in heart put them away. You have resolved to give yourself to God. Now go to Him, and ask that He will wash away your sins, and give you a new heart. Then believe that He does this *because He has promised*. This is the lesson which Jesus taught while He was on earth, that the gift which God promises us, we must believe we do receive, and it is ours. Jesus healed the people of their diseases when they had faith in His power; He helped them in the things which they could see, thus inspiring them with confidence in Him concerning things which they could not see—leading them to believe in His power to forgive sins. This He plainly stated in the healing of the man sick with palsy: *"That ye may know that the Son of man hath power on earth to forgive sins* (then saith He to the sick of the palsy), Arise, take up thy bed, and go unto thine house."* Matthew 9:6. So also John the evangelist says, speaking of the miracles of Christ, "These are written, that ye might believe that Jesus is the Christ, the Son of God; and that believing ye might have life through His name." John 20:31.

From the simple Bible account of how Jesus healed the sick, we may learn something about how to believe in Him for the forgiveness of sins. Let us turn to the story of the paralytic at Bethesda. The poor sufferer was helpless; he had not used his limbs for thirty-eight years. Yet Jesus bade him, "Rise, take up thy bed, and walk." Tho sick man might have said, "Lord, if Thou wilt make me whole, I will obey Thy word." But no, he believed Christ's word, believed that he was made whole, and he made the effort at once; he *willed* to walk, and he did walk. He acted on the word of Christ, and God gave the power. He was made whole.

In like manner you are a sinner. You cannot atone for your past sins, you cannot change your heart, and make yourself holy. But God promises to do all this for you through Christ. You *believe* that promise. You confess your sins, and give yourself to God. You *will* to serve Him. Just as surely as you do this, God will fulfill His word to you. If you believe the promise—believe that you are forgiven and cleansed—God supplies the fact; you are made whole, just as Christ gave the paralytic power to walk when the man believed that he was healed. It *is* so, if you believe it.

Do not wait to *feel* that you are made whole, but say, "I believe it; it *is* so, not because I feel it, but because God has promised."

Jesus says, "What things soever ye desire, when ye

pray, believe that ye receive them, and ye shall have them." Mark 11:24. There is a condition to this promise—that we pray according to the will of God. But it is the will of God to cleanse us from sin, to make us His children, and to enable us to live a holy life. So we may ask for these blessings, and believe that we receive them, and thank God that we *have* received them. It is our privilege to go to Jesus and be cleansed, and to stand before the law without shame or remorse. "There is therefore now no condemnation to them which are in Christ Jesus, who walk not after the flesh, but after the Spirit." Romans 8:1.

Henceforth you are not your own; you are bought with a price. "Ye were not redeemed with corruptible things, as silver and gold, . . . but with the precious blood of Christ, as of a lamb without blemish and without spot." 1 Peter 1:18, 19. Through this simple act of believing God, the Holy Spirit has begotten a new life in your heart. You are as a child born into the family of God, and He loves you as He loves His Son.

Now that you have given yourself to Jesus, do not draw back, do not take yourself away from Him, but day by day say, "I am Christ's; I have given myself to Him;" and ask Him to give you His Spirit, and keep you by His grace. As it is by giving yourself to God, and believing Him, that you become His child, so you are to live in Him. The apostle says, "As ye have therefore received Christ Jesus the Lord, so walk ye in Him." Colossians 2:6.

Some seem to feel that they must be on probation, and must prove to the Lord that they are reformed, before they can claim His blessing. But they may claim the blessing of God even now. They must have His grace, the Spirit of Christ, to help their infirmities, or they cannot resist evil. Jesus loves to have us come to Him just as we are, sinful, helpless, dependent. We may come with all our weakness, our folly, our sinfulness, and fall at His feet in penitence. It is His glory to encircle us in the arms of His love, and to bind up our wounds, to cleanse us from all impurity.

Here is where thousands fail: they do not believe that Jesus pardons them personally, individually. They do not take God at His word. It is the privilege of all who comply with the conditions to know for themselves that pardon is freely extended for every sin. Put away the suspicion that God's promises are not meant for you. They are for every repentant transgressor. Strength and grace have been provided through Christ to be brought by ministering angels to every believing soul. None are so sinful that they cannot find strength, purity, and righteousness in Jesus, who died for them. He is waiting to strip them of their garments stained and polluted with sin, and to put upon them the white robes of righteousness; He bids them live and not die.

God does not deal with us as finite men deal with one another. His thoughts are thoughts of mercy, love, and tenderest compassion. He says, "Let the wicked forsake his way, and the unrighteous man his thoughts; and let him return unto the Lord, and He will have mercy upon him; and to our God, for He will abundantly pardon." "I have blotted out, as a thick cloud, thy transgression, and, as a cloud, thy sins." Isaiah 55:7; 44:22.

"I have no pleasure in the death of him that dieth, saith the Lord God: wherefore turn yourselves, and live ye." Ezekiel 18:32. Satan is ready to steal away the blessed assurances of God. He desires to take every glimmer of hope and every ray of light from the soul; but you must not permit him to do this. Do not give ear to the tempter, but say: "Jesus has died that I might live. He loves me, and wills not that I should perish. I have a compassionate heavenly Father; and although I have abused His love, though the blessings He has given me have been squandered, I will arise, and go to my Father, and say, 'I have sinned against heaven, and before Thee, and am no more worthy to be called Thy son: make me as one of Thy hired servants.'" The parable tells you how the wanderer will be received: *"When he was yet a great way off,* his father saw him, and had compassion, and ran, and fell on his neck, and kissed him." Luke 15:18-20.

But even this parable, tender and touching as it is, comes short of expressing the infinite compassion of the heavenly Father. The Lord declares by His prophet, "I have loved thee with an everlasting love: *therefore with loving—kindness have I drawn thee.*" Jeremiah 31:3. While the sinner is yet far from the Father's house, wasting his substance in a strange country, the Father's heart is yearning over him; and every longing awakened in the soul to return to God, is but the tender pleading of His Spirit, wooing, entreating, drawing the wanderer to his Father's heart of love.

With the rich promises of the Bible before you, can you give place to doubt? Can you believe that when the poor sinner longs to return, longs to forsake his sins, the Lord sternly withholds him from coming to His feet in repentance? Away with such thoughts! Nothing can hurt your own soul more than to entertain such a conception of our heavenly Father. He hates sin, but He loves the sinner, and He gave Himself in the person of Christ, that all who would might be saved, and have eternal blessedness in the kingdom of glory. What stronger or more tender language could have been employed than He has chosen in which to express His love toward us? He declares, "Can a woman forget her sucking child, that she should not have compassion on the son of her womb? Yea, they may forget, yet will I not forget thee." Isaiah 49:15.

Look up, you that are doubting and trembling; for Jesus lives to make intercession for us. Thank God for the gift of His dear Son, and pray that He may not have died for you in vain. The Spirit invites you today. Come with your whole heart to Jesus, and you may claim His blessing.

As you read the promises, remember they are the expression of unutterable love and pity. The great heart of Infinite Love is drawn toward the sinner with boundless compassion. "We have redemption through His blood, the forgiveness of sins." Ephesians 1:7. Yes, only believe that God is your helper. He wants to restore His moral image in man. As you draw near to Him with confession and repentance, He will draw near to you with mercy and forgiveness.

CHAPTER 7

THE ACID TEST

"IF ANY MAN be in Christ, he is a new creature: old things are passed away; behold, all things are become new." 2 Corinthians 5:17.

A person may not be able to tell the exact time or place, or trace all the chain of circumstances in the process of conversion; but this does not prove him to be unconverted. Christ said to Nicodemus, "The wind bloweth where it listeth, and thou hearest the sound thereof, but canst not tell whence it cometh, and whither it goeth: so is everyone that is born of the Spirit." John 3:8. Like the wind, which is invisible, yet the effects of which are plainly seen and felt, is the Spirit of God in its work upon the human heart. That regenerating power, which no human eye can see, begets a new life in the soul; it creates a new being in the image of God. While the work of the Spirit is silent and imperceptible, its effects are manifest. If the heart has been renewed by the Spirit of God, the life will bear witness to the fact. While we cannot do anything to change our hearts, or to bring ourselves into harmony with God; while we must not trust at all to ourselves or our good works, our lives will reveal whether the grace of God is dwelling within us. A change will be seen in the character, the habits, the pursuits. The contrast will be clear and decided between what they have been and what they are. The character is revealed, not by occasional good deeds and occasional misdeeds, but by the tendency of the habitual words and acts.

It is true that there may be an outward correctness of deportment without the renewing power of Christ. The love of influence and the desire for the esteem of others may produce a well-ordered life. Self-respect may lead us to avoid the appearance of evil. A selfish heart may perform generous actions. By what means, then, shall we determine whose side we are on?

Who has the heart? With whom are our thoughts? Of whom do we love to converse? Who has our warmest affections and our best energies? If we are Christ's, our thoughts are with Him, and our sweetest thoughts are of Him. All we have and are is consecrated to Him. We long to bear His image, breathe His spirit, do His will, and please Him in all things.

Those who become new creatures in Christ Jesus will bring forth the fruits of the Spirit, "love, joy, peace, long-suffering, gentleness, goodness, faith, meekness, temperance." Galatians 5:22, 23. They will no longer fashion themselves according to the former lusts, but by the faith of the Son of God they will follow in His steps, reflect His character, and purify themselves even as He is pure. The things they once hated, they now love; and the things they once loved, they hate. The proud and self-assertive become meek and lowly in heart. The vain and supercilious become serious and unobtrusive. The drunken become sober, and the profligate pure. The vain customs and fashions of the world are laid aside. Christians will seek not the "outward adorning," but "the hidden man of the heart, in that which is not corruptible, even the ornament of a meek and quiet spirit." 1 Peter 3:3, 4.

There is no evidence of genuine repentance, unless it works reformation. If he restore the pledge, give again that he had robbed, confess his sins, and love God and his fellow men, the sinner may be sure that he has passed from death unto life.

When, as erring, sinful beings, we come to Christ and become partakers of His pardoning grace, love springs up in the heart. Every burden is light; for the yoke that Christ imposes is easy. Duty becomes a delight, and sacrifice a pleasure. The path that seemed shrouded in darkness, becomes bright with beams from the Sun of

Righteousness.

The loveliness of the character of Christ will be seen in His followers. It was His delight to do the will of God. Love to God, zeal for His glory, was the controlling power in our Saviour's life. Love beautified and ennobled all His actions. Love is of God. The unconsecrated heart cannot originate or produce it. It is found only in the heart where Jesus reigns. "We love, because He first loved us." 1 John 4:19, R.V. In the heart renewed by divine grace, love is the principle of action. It modifies the character, governs the impulses, controls the passions, subdues enmity, and ennobles the affections. This love, cherished in the soul, sweetens the life, and sheds a refining influence on all around.

There are two errors against which the children of God—particularly those who have just come to trust in His grace—especially need to guard. The first, already dwelt upon, is that of looking to their own works, trusting to anything they can do, to bring themselves into harmony with God. He who is trying to become holy by his own works in keeping the law, is attempting an impossibility. All that man can do without Christ is polluted with selfishness and sin. It is the grace of Christ alone, through faith, that can make us holy.

The opposite and no less dangerous error is, that belief in Christ releases men from keeping the law of God; that since by faith alone we become partakers of the grace of Christ, our works have nothing to do with our redemption.

But notice here that obedience is not a mere outward compliance, but the service of love. The law of God is an expression of His very nature; it is an embodiment of the great principle of love, and hence is the foundation of His government in heaven and earth. If our hearts are renewed in the likeness of God, if the divine love is implanted in the soul, will not the law of God be carried out in the life? When the principle of love is implanted in the heart, when man is renewed after the image of Him that created him, the new-covenant promise is fulfilled, "I will put My laws

into their hearts, and in their minds will I write them."
Hebrews 10:16. And if the law is written in the heart,
will it not shape the life? Obedience—the service and
allegiance of love—is the true sign of discipleship. Thus
the Scripture says, "This is the love of God, that we keep
His commandments." "He that saith, I know Him, and
keepeth not His commandments, is a liar, and the truth is
not in him." 1 John 5:3; 2:4. Instead of releasing man
from obedience, it is faith, and faith only, that makes us
partakers of the grace of Christ, which enables us to render
obedience.

We do not earn salvation by our obedience; for
salvation is the free gift of God, to be received by faith.
But obedience is the fruit of faith. "Ye know that He was
manifested to take away our sins; and in Him is no sin.
Whosoever abideth in Him sinneth not; whosoever
sinneth hath not seen Him, neither known Him." 1 John
3:5, 6. Here is the true test. If we abide in Christ, if the
love of God dwells in us, our feelings, our thoughts, our
purposes, our actions, will be in harmony with the will of
God as expressed in the precepts of His holy law. "Little
children, let no man deceive you: he that doeth
righteousness is righteous, even as He is righteous." 1
John 3:7. Righteousness is defined by the standard of
God's holy law, as expressed in the ten precepts given on
Sinai.

That so-called faith in Christ which professes to
release men from the obligation of obedience of God, is
not faith, but presumption. "By grace are ye saved
through faith." But "faith, if it hath not works, is dead."
Ephesians 2:8; James 2:17. Jesus said of Himself before
He came to earth, "I delight to do Thy will, O My God;
yea, Thy law is within My heart." Psalm 40:8. And just
before He ascended again to heaven He declared, "I have
kept My Father's commandments, and abide in His love."
John 15:10. The Scripture says, "Hereby we do know
that we know Him, if we keep His commandments.... He
that saith he abideth in Him ought himself also so to
walk, even as He walked." 1 John 2:3, 6. "Because

Christ also suffered for us, leaving us an example, that ye should follow His steps." 1 Peter 2:21.

The condition of eternal life is now just what it always has been—just what it was in Paradise before the fall of our first parents—perfect obedience to the law of God, perfect righteousness. If eternal life were granted on any condition short of this, then the happiness of the whole universe would be imperiled. The way would be open for sin, with all its train of woe and misery, to be immortalized.

It was possible for Adam, before the fall, to form a righteous character by obedience to God's law. But he failed to do this, and because of his sin our natures are fallen, and we cannot make ourselves righteous. Since we are sinful, unholy, we cannot perfectly obey the holy law. We have no righteousness of our own with which to meet the claims of the law of God. But Christ has made a way of escape for us. He lived on earth amid trials and temptations such as we have to meet. He lived a sinless life. He died for us, and now He offers to take our sins and give us His righteousness. If you give yourself to Him, and accept Him as your Saviour, then, sinful as your life may have been, for His sake you are accounted righteous. Christ's character stands in place of your character, and you are accepted before God just as if you had not sinned.

More than this, Christ changes the heart. He abides in your heart by faith. You are to maintain this connection with Christ by faith and the continual surrender of your will to Him; and so long as you do this, He will work in you to will and to do according to His good pleasure. So you may say, "The life which I now live in the flesh I live by the faith of the Son of God, who loved me, and gave Himself for me." Galatians 2:20. So Jesus said to His disciples, "It is not ye that speak, but the Spirit of your Father which speaketh in you." Matthew 10:20. Then with Christ working in you, you will manifest the same spirit and do the same good works—works of righteousness, obedience.

So we have nothing in ourselves of which to boast. We have no ground for self-exaltation. Our only ground of hope is in the righteousness of Christ imputed to us, and in that wrought by His Spirit working in and through us.

When we speak of faith, there is a distinction that should be borne in mind. There is a kind of belief that is wholly distinct from faith. The existence and power of God, the truth of His Word, are facts that even Satan and his hosts cannot at heart deny. The Bible says that "the devils also believe and tremble" (James 2:19); but this is not faith. Where there is not only a belief in God's Word, but a submission of the will to Him; where the heart is yielded to Him, the affections fixed upon Him, there is faith—faith that works by love, and purifies the soul. Through this faith the heart is renewed in the image of God. And the heart that in its unrenewed state is not subject to the law of God, neither indeed can be, now delights in its holy precepts, exclaiming with the psalmist, "O how love I Thy law! it is my meditation all the day." Psalm 119:97. And the righteousness of the law is fulfilled in us, "who walk not after the flesh, but after the Spirit." Romans 8:1.

There are those who have known the pardoning love of Christ, and who really desire to be children of God, yet they realize that their character is imperfect, their life faulty, and they are ready to doubt whether their hearts have been renewed by the Holy Spirit. To such I would say, Do not draw back in despair. We shall often have to bow down and weep at the feet of Jesus because of our shortcomings and mistakes; but we are not to be discouraged. Even if we are overcome by the enemy, we are not cast off, not forsaken and rejected of God. No; Christ is at the right hand of God, who also maketh intercession for us. Said the beloved John, "These things write I unto you, that ye sin not. And if any man sin, we have an advocate with the Father, Jesus Christ the righteous." 1 John 2:1. And do not forget the words of Christ, "The Father Himself loveth you." John 16:27.

He desires to restore you to Himself, to see His own purity and holiness reflected in you. And if you will but yield yourself to Him, He that hath begun a good work in you will carry it forward to the day of Jesus Christ. Pray more fervently; believe more fully. As we come to distrust our own power, let us trust the power of our Redeemer, and we shall praise Him who is the health of our countenance.

The closer you come to Jesus, the more faulty you will appear in your own eyes; for your vision will be clearer, and your imperfections will be seen in broad and distinct contrast to His perfect nature. This is evidence that Satan's delusions have lost their power; that the vivifying influence of the Spirit of God is arousing you.

No deep-seated love for Jesus can dwell in the heart that does not realize its own sinfulness. The soul that is transformed by the grace of Christ will admire His divine character; but if we do not see our own moral deformity, it is unmistakable evidence that we have not had a view of the beauty and excellence of Christ.

The less we see to esteem in ourselves, the more we shall see to esteem in the infinite purity and loveliness of our Saviour. A view of our sinfulness drives us to Him who can pardon; and when the soul, realizing its helplessness, reaches out after Christ, He will reveal Himself in power. The more our sense of need drives us to Him and to the Word of God, the more exalted views we shall have of His character, and the more fully we shall reflect His image.

CHAPTER 8

MEASURING UP

THE CHANGE OF HEART by which we become children of God is in the Bible spoken of as birth. Again, it is compared to the germination of the good seed sown by the husbandman. In like manner those who are just converted to Christ are, as "newborn babes," to "grow up" (1 Peter 2:2; Ephesians 4:15) to the stature of men and women in Christ Jesus. Or like the good seed sown in the field, they are to grow up and bring forth fruit. Isaiah says that they shall "be called trees of righteousness, the planting of the Lord, that He might be glorified." Isaiah 61:3. So from natural life, illustrations are drawn, to help us better to understand the mysterious truths of spiritual life.

Not all the wisdom and skill of man can produce life in the smallest object in nature. It is only through the life which God Himself has imparted, that either plant or animal can live. So it is only through the life from God that spiritual life is begotten in the hearts of men. Unless a man is "born from above," (John 3:3, margin), he cannot become a partaker of the life which Christ came to give.

As with life, so it is with growth. It is God who brings the bud to bloom and the flower to fruit. It is by His power that the seed develops, "first the blade, then the ear, after that the full corn in the ear." Mark 4:28. And the prophet Hosea says of Israel, that "he shall grow as the lily." "They shall revive as the corn, and grow as the vine." Hosea 14:5, 7. And Jesus bids us "consider the lilies how they grow." Luke 12:27. The plants and flowers grow not by their own care or anxiety or effort, but by receiving that which God has furnished to minister to their life. The child cannot, by any anxiety or power of its own, add to its stature. No more can you, by anxiety or effort of yourself, secure spiritual growth. The plant, the child, grows by receiving from its surroundings that which ministers to its life—air, sunshine, and food. What these gifts of nature are to animal and plant, such is Christ to those who trust in Him. He is their "everlasting light," "a sun and shield." Isaiah 60:19; Psalm 84:11. He shall be as "the dew unto Israel." "He shall come down like rain upon the mown grass." Hosea 14:5; Psalm 72:6. He is the living water, "the bread of God . . which cometh down from heaven, and giveth life unto the world." John 6:33.

In the matchless gift of His Son, God has encircled the whole world with an atmosphere of grace as real as the air which circulates around the globe. All who choose to breathe this life-giving atmosphere will live, and grow up to the stature of men and women in Christ Jesus.

As the flower turns to the sun, that the bright beams may aid in perfecting its beauty and symmetry, so should we turn to the Sun of Righteousness, that heaven's light may shine upon us, that our character may be developed into the likeness of Christ.

Jesus teaches the same thing when He says, "Abide in Me, and I in you. As the branch cannot bear fruit of itself, except it abide in the vine; no more can ye, except ye abide in Me.... Without Me ye can do nothing." John 15:4, 5. You are just as dependent upon Christ, in order to live a holy life, as is the branch upon the parent stock for growth and fruitfulness. Apart from Him you have no life. You have no power to resist temptation or to grow in grace and holiness. Abiding in Him, you may flourish. Drawing your life from Him, you will not wither nor be fruitless. You will be like a tree planted by the rivers of water.

Many have an idea that they must do some part of the work alone. They have trusted in Christ for the forgiveness of sin, but now they seek by their own efforts to live aright. But every such effort must fail. Jesus says, "Without Me ye can do nothing." Our growth in grace, our joy, our usefulness—all depend upon our union with Christ. It is by communion with Him, daily, hourly—by abiding in Him—that we are to grow in grace. He is not only the Author but the Finisher of our faith. It is Christ first and last and always. He is to be with us, not only at the beginning and the end of our course, but at every step of the way. David says, "I have set the Lord always before me: because He is at my right hand, I shall not be moved." Psalm 16:8.

Do you ask, "How am I to abide in Christ?" In the same way as you received Him at first. "As we have therefore received Christ Jesus the Lord, so walk ye in Him." "The just shall live by faith." Colossians 2:6; Hebrews 10:38. You gave yourself to God, to be His wholly, to serve and obey Him, and you took Christ as your Saviour. You could not yourself atone for your sins or change your heart; but having given yourself to God, you believed that He for Christ's sake did all this for you. By *faith* you became Christ's, and by faith you are to grow up in Him—by giving and taking. You are to *give* all—your heart, your will, your service—give yourself to Him to obey all His requirements; and you must *take* all—Christ, the fullness of all blessing, to abide in your heart, to be your strength, your righteousness, your everlasting helper—to give you power to obey.

Consecrate yourself to God in the morning; make this your very first work. Let your prayer be, "Take me, O Lord, as wholly Thine. I lay all my plans at Thy feet. Use me today in Thy service. Abide with me, and let all my work be wrought in Thee." This is a daily matter. Each morning consecrate yourself to God for that day. Surrender all your plans to Him, to be carried out or given up as His providence shall indicate. Thus day by day you may be giving your life into the hands of God, and thus your life will be molded more and more after the life of Christ.

A life in Christ is a life of restfulness. There may be no ecstasy of feeling, but there should be an abiding, peaceful trust. Your hope is not in yourself; it is in Christ. Your weakness is united to His strength, your ignorance to His wisdom, your frailty to His enduring might. So you are not to look to yourself, not to let the mind dwell upon self, but look to Christ. Let the mind dwell upon His love, upon the beauty, the perfection, of His character. Christ in His self-denial, Christ in His humiliation, Christ in His purity and holiness, Christ in His matchless love—this is the subject for the soul's contemplation. It is by loving Him, copying Him, depending wholly upon Him, that you are to be transformed into His likeness.

Jesus says, "Abide in Me." These words convey the idea of rest, stability, confidence. Again He invites, "Come unto Me, . . . and I will give you rest." Matthew 11:28, 29. The words of the psalmist express the same thought: "Rest in the Lord, and wait patiently for Him." And Isaiah gives the assurance, "In quietness and confidence shall be your strength." Psalm 37:7; Isaiah 30:15. This rest is not found in inactivity; for in the Saviour's invitation the promise of rest is united with the call to labor: "Take My yoke upon you, . . . and ye shall find rest." Matthew 11:29. The heart that rests most fully upon Christ will be most earnest and active in labor for Him.

When the mind dwells upon self, it is turned away from Christ, the source of strength and life. Hence it is Satan's constant effort to keep the attention diverted from the Saviour, and thus prevent the union and communion of the soul with Christ. The pleasures of the world, life's cares and perplexities and sorrows, the faults of others, or your own faults and imperfections—to any or all of these he will seek to divert the mind. Do not be misled by his devices. Many who are really conscientious, and who desire to live for God, he too often leads to dwell upon their own faults and weaknesses, and thus by separating them from Christ, he hopes to gain the victory. We should not make self the center, and indulge anxiety and fear as to whether we shall be saved. All this turns the soul away from the Source of our strength. Commit the keeping of your soul to God, and trust in Him. Talk and think of Jesus. Let self be lost in Him. Put away all doubt; dismiss your fears. Say with the apostle Paul, "I live; yet not I, but Christ liveth in me: and the life which I now live in the flesh I live by the faith of the Son of God, who loved me, and gave Himself for me." Galatians 2:20. Rest in God. He is able to keep that which you have committed to Him. If you will leave yourself in His hands, He will bring you off more than conqueror through Him that has loved you.

When Christ took human nature upon Him, He bound humanity to Himself by a tie of love that can never be broken by any power save the choice of man himself. Satan will constantly present allurements to induce us to break this tie—to choose to separate ourselves from Christ. Here is where we need to watch, to strive, to pray, that nothing may entice us to *choose* another master; for we are always free to do this. But let us keep our eyes fixed upon Christ, and He will preserve us. Looking unto Jesus, we are safe. Nothing can pluck us out of His hand. In constantly beholding Him, we "are changed into the same image from glory to glory, even as by the Spirit of the Lord." 2 Corinthians 3:18.

It was thus that the early disciples gained their likeness to the dear Saviour. When those disciples heard the words of Jesus, they felt their need of Him. They sought, they found, they followed Him. They were with Him in the house, at the table, in the closet, in the field. They were with Him as pupils with a teacher, daily receiving from His lips lessons of holy truth. They looked to Him, as servants to their master, to learn their duty. Those disciples were men "subject to like passions as we are." James 5:17. They had the same battle with sin to fight. They needed the same grace, in order to live a holy life.

Even John, the beloved disciple, the one who most fully reflected the likeness of the Saviour, did not naturally possess that loveliness of character. He was not only self-assertive and ambitious for honor, but impetuous, and resentful under injuries. But as the character of the Divine One was manifested to him, he saw his own deficiency, and was humbled by the knowledge. The strength and patience, the power and tenderness, the majesty and meekness, that he beheld in the daily life of the Son of God, filled his soul with admiration and love. Day by day his heart was drawn out toward Christ, until he lost sight of self in love for his Master. His resentful, ambitious temper was yielded to the molding power of Christ. The regenerating influence of the Holy Spirit renewed his heart. The power of the love of Christ wrought a transformation of character. This is the sure result of union with Jesus. When Christ abides in the heart, the whole nature is transformed. Christ's Spirit, His love, softens the heart, subdues the soul, and raises the thoughts and desires toward God and heaven.

When Christ ascended to heaven, the sense of His presence was still with His followers. It was a personal presence, full of love and light. Jesus, the Saviour, who had walked and talked and prayed with them, who had spoken hope and comfort to their hearts, had, while the message of peace was still upon His lips, been taken up from them into heaven, and the tones of His voice had come back to them, as the cloud of angels received Him— "Lo, I am with you alway, even unto the end of the world." Matthew 28:20. He had ascended to heaven in the form of humanity. They knew that He was before the throne of God, their Friend and Saviour still; that His sympathies were unchanged; that He was still identified with suffering humanity. He was presenting before God the merits of His own precious blood, showing His wounded hands and feet, in remembrance of the price He had paid for His redeemed. They knew that He had ascended to heaven to prepare places for them, and that He would come again, and take them to Himself.

As they met together, after the ascension, they were eager to present their requests to the Father in the name of

Jesus. In solemn awe they bowed in prayer, repeating the assurance, "Whatsoever ye shall ask the Father in My name, He will give it you. Hitherto have ye asked nothing in My name: ask, and ye shall receive, that your joy may be full." John 16:23, 24. They extended the hand of faith higher and higher, with the mighty argument, "It is Christ that died, yea rather, that is risen again, who is even at the right hand of God, who also maketh intercession for us." Romans 8:34. And Pentecost brought them the presence of the Comforter, of whom Christ had said, He "shall be in you." And He had further said, "It is expedient for you that I go away: for if I go not away, the Comforter will not come unto you; but if I depart, I will send Him unto you." John 14:17; 16:7. Henceforth through the Spirit, Christ was to abide continually in the hearts of His children. Their union with Him was closer than when He was personally with them. The light, and love, and power of the indwelling Christ shone out through them, so that men, beholding, "marveled; and they took knowledge of them, that they had been with Jesus." Acts 4:13.

All that Christ was to the disciples, He desires to be to His children today; for in that last prayer, with the little band of disciples gathered about Him, He said, "Neither pray I for these alone, but for them also which shall believe on Me through their word." John 17:20.

Jesus prayed for us, and He asked that we might be one with Him, even as He is one with the Father. What a union is this! The Saviour has said of Himself, "The Son can do nothing of Himself;" "the Father that dwelleth in Me, He doeth the works." John 5:19; 14:10. Then if Christ is dwelling in our hearts, He will work in us "both to will and to do of His good pleasure." Philippians 2:13. We shall work as He worked; we shall manifest the same spirit. And thus, loving Him and abiding in Him, we shall "grow up into Him in all things, which is the head, even Christ." Ephesians 4:15.

CHAPTER 9

"GIVING" MEANS LIVING

GOD IS THE SOURCE of life and light and joy to the universe. Like rays of light from the sun, like the streams of water bursting from a living spring, blessings flow out from Him to all His creatures. And wherever the life of God is in the hearts of men, it will flow out to others in love and blessing.

Our Saviour's joy was in the uplifting and redemption of fallen men. For this He counted not His life dear unto Himself, but endured the cross, despising the shame. So angels are ever engaged in working for the happiness of others. This is their joy. That which selfish hearts would regard as humiliating service, ministering to those who are wretched and in every way inferior in character and rank, is the work of sinless angels. The spirit of Christ's self-sacrificing love is the spirit that pervades heaven, and is the very essence of its bliss. This is the spirit that Christ's followers will possess, the work that they will do.

When the love of Christ is enshrined in the heart, like sweet fragrance it cannot be hidden. Its holy influence will be felt by all with whom we come in contact. The spirit of Christ in the heart is like a spring in the desert, flowing to refresh all, and making those who are ready to perish, eager to drink of the water of life.

Love to Jesus will be manifested in a desire to work as He worked, for the blessing and uplifting of humanity. It will lead to love, tenderness, and sympathy toward all the creatures of our heavenly Father's care.

The Saviour's life on earth was not a life of ease and devotion to Himself, but He toiled with persistent, earnest, untiring effort for the salvation of lost mankind.

From the manger to Calvary He followed the path of self-denial, and sought not to be released from arduous tasks, painful travels, and exhausting care and labor. He said, "The Son of man came not to be ministered unto, but to minister, and to give His life a ransom for many." Matthew 20:28. This was the one great object of His life. Everything else was secondary and subservient. It was His meat and drink to do the will of God and to finish His work. Self and self-interest had no part in His labor.

So those who are the partakers of the grace of Christ will be ready to make any sacrifice, that others for whom He died may share the heavenly gift. They will do all they can to make the world better for their stay in it. This spirit is the sure outgrowth of a soul truly converted. No sooner does one come to Christ, than there is born in his heart a desire to make known to others what a precious friend he has found in Jesus; the saving and sanctifying truth cannot be shut up in his heart. If we are clothed with the righteousness of Christ, and are filled with the joy of His indwelling Spirit, we shall not be able to hold our peace. If we have tasted and seen that the Lord is good, we shall have something to tell. Like Philip when he found the Saviour, we shall invite others into His presence. We shall seek to present to them the attractions of Christ, and the unseen realities of the world to come. There will be an intensity of desire to follow in the path that Jesus trod. There will be an earnest longing that those around us may behold "the Lamb of God, which taketh away the sin of the world." John 1:29.

And the effort to bless others will react in blessings upon ourselves. This was the purpose of God in giving us a part to act in the plan of redemption. He has granted men the privilege of becoming partakers of the divine nature, and, in their turn, of diffusing blessings to their fellow men. This is the highest honor, the greatest joy, that it is possible for God to bestow upon men. Those who thus become participants in labors of love are brought nearest to their Creator.

God might have committed the message of the

gospel, and all the work of loving ministry, to the heavenly angels. He might have employed other means for accomplishing His purpose. But in His infinite love He chose to make us co-workers with Himself, with Christ and the angels, that we might share the blessing, the joy, the spiritual uplifting, which results from this unselfish ministry.

We are brought into sympathy with Christ through the fellowship of His sufferings. Every act of self-sacrifice for the good of others strengthens the spirit of beneficence in the giver's heart, allying him more closely to the Redeemer of the world, who "was rich, yet for your sakes . . . became poor, that ye through His poverty might be rich." 2 Corinthians 8:9. And it is only as we thus fulfill the divine purpose in our creation, that life can be a blessing to us.

If you will go to work as Christ designs that His disciples shall, and win souls for Him, you will feel the need of a deeper experience and a greater knowledge in divine things, and will hunger and thirst after righteousness. You will plead with God, and your faith will be strengthened, and your soul will drink deeper drafts at the well of salvation. Encountering opposition and trials will drive you to the Bible and prayer. You will grow in grace and the knowledge of Christ, and will develop a rich experience.

The spirit of unselfish labor for others gives depth, stability, and Christlike loveliness to the character, and brings peace and happiness to its possessor. The aspirations are elevated. There is no room for sloth or selfishness. Those who thus exercise the Christian graces will grow, and will become strong to work for God. They will have clear spiritual perceptions, a steady, growing faith, and an increased power in prayer. The Spirit of God, moving upon their spirit, calls forth the sacred harmonies of the soul, in answer to the divine touch. Those who thus devote themselves to unselfish effort for the good of others, are most surely working out their own salvation.

The only way to grow in grace is to be disinterestedly doing the very work which Christ has enjoined upon us—to engage, to the extent of our ability, in helping and blessing those who need the help we can give them. Strength comes by exercise; activity is the very condition of life. Those who endeavor to maintain Christian life by passively accepting the blessings that come through the means of grace, and doing nothing for Christ, are simply trying to live by eating without working. And in the spiritual as in the natural world, this always results in degeneration and decay. A man who would refuse to exercise his limbs would soon lose all power to use them. Thus the Christian who will not exercise his God-given powers, not only fails to grow up into Christ, but he loses the strength that he already had.

The church of Christ is God's appointed agency for the salvation of men. Its mission is to carry the gospel to the world. And the obligation rests upon all Christians. Every one, to the extent of his talent and opportunity, is to fulfill the Saviour's commission. The love of Christ, revealed to us, makes us debtors to all who know Him not. God has given us light, not for ourselves alone, but to shed upon them.

If the followers of Christ were awake to duty, there would be thousands where there is one today, proclaiming the gospel in heathen lands. And all who could not personally engage in the work, would yet sustain it with their means, their sympathy, and their prayers. And there would be far more earnest labor for souls in Christian countries.

We need not go to heathen lands, or even leave the narrow circle of the home, if it is there that our duty lies, in order to work for Christ. We can do this in the home circle, in the church, among those with whom we associate, and with whom we do business.

The greater part of our Saviour's life on earth was spent in patient toil in the carpenter's shop at Nazareth. Ministering angels attended the Lord of life as He walked side by side with peasants and laborers, unrecognized and unhonored. He was as faithfully fulfilling His mission while working at His humble trade as when He healed the sick or walked upon the storm-tossed waves of Galilee. So, in the humblest duties and lowliest positions of life, we may walk and work with Jesus.

The apostle says, "Let every man, wherein he is called, therein abide with God." 1 Corinthians 7:24. The businessman may conduct his business in a way that will glorify his Master because of his fidelity. If he is a true follower of Christ, he will carry his religion into everything that is done, and reveal to men the spirit of Christ. The mechanic may be a diligent and faithful representative of Him who toiled in the lowly walks of life among the hills of Galilee. Everyone who names the name of Christ should so work that others, by seeing his good works, may be led to glorify their Creator and Redeemer.

Many have excused themselves from rendering their gifts to the service of Christ, because others were possessed of superior endowments and advantages. The opinion has prevailed that only those who are especially talented are required to consecrate their abilities to the service of God. It has come to be understood by many that talents are given to only a certain favored class, to the exclusion of others, who of course, are not called upon to share in the toils or the rewards. But it is not so represented in the parable. When the master of the house called his servants, he gave to every man *his* work.

With a loving spirit we may perform life's humblest duties "as to the Lord." Colossians 3:23. If the love of God is in the heart, it will be manifested in the life. The sweet savor of Christ will surround us, and our influence will elevate and bless.

You are not to wait for great occasions or to expect extraordinary abilities before you go to work for God. You need not have a thought of what the world will think of you. If your daily life is a testimony to the purity and sincerity of your faith, and others are convinced that you desire to benefit them, your efforts will not be wholly lost.

The humblest and poorest of the disciples of Jesus can be a blessing to others. They may not realize that they are doing any special good, but by their unconscious influence they may start waves of blessing that will widen and deepen, and the blessed results they may never know until the day of final reward. They do not feel or know that they are doing anything great. They are not required to weary themselves with anxiety about success. They have only to go forward quietly, doing faithfully the work that God's providence assigns, and their life will not be in vain. Their own souls will be growing more and more into the likeness of Christ; they are workers together with God in this life, and are thus fitting for the higher work and the unshadowed joy of the life to come.

CHAPTER 10

LISTEN TO GOD

MANY ARE THE WAYS in which God is seeking to make Himself known to us and bring us into communion with Him. Nature speaks to our senses without ceasing. The open heart will be impressed with the love and glory of God as revealed through the words of His hands. The listening ear can hear and understand the communications of God through the things of nature. The green fields, the lofty trees, the buds and flowers, the passing cloud, the falling rain, the babbling brook, the glories of the heavens, speak to our hearts, and invite us to become acquainted with Him who made them all.

Our Saviour bound up His precious lessons with the things of nature. The trees, the birds, the flowers of the valleys, the hills, the lakes, and the beautiful heavens, as well as the incidents and surroundings of daily life, were all linked with the words of truth, that His lessons might thus be often recalled to mind, even amid the busy cares of man's life of toil.

God would have His children appreciate His works, and delight in the simple, quiet beauty with which He has adorned our earthly home. He is a lover of the beautiful, and above all that is outwardly attractive He loves beauty of character; He would have us cultivate purity and simplicity, the quiet graces of the flowers.

If we will but listen, God's created works will teach us precious lessons of obedience and trust. From the stars that in their trackless courses through space follow from age to age their appointed path, down to the minutest atom, the things of nature obey the Creator's will. And God cares for everything and sustains everything that He has created. He who upholds the unnumbered worlds throughout immensity, at the same time cares for the wants of the little brown sparrow that sings its humble song without fear. When men go forth to their daily toil, as when they engage in prayer; when they lie down at night, and when they rise in the morning; when the rich man feasts in his palace, or when the poor man gathers his children about the scanty board, each is tenderly watched by the heavenly Father. No tears are shed that God does not notice. There is no smile that He does not mark.

If we would but fully believe this, all undue anxieties would be dismissed. Our lives would not be so filled with disappointment as now; for everything, whether great or small, would be left in the hands of God, who is not perplexed by the multiplicity of cares, or overwhelmed by their weight. We should then enjoy a rest of soul to which many have long been strangers.

As your senses delight in the attractive loveliness of the earth, think of the world that is to come, that shall never know the blight of sin and death; where the face of nature will no more wear the shadow of the curse. Let your imagination picture the home of the saved, and remember that it will be more glorious than your brightest imagination can portray. In the varied gifts of God in nature we see but the faintest gleaming of His glory. It is written, "Eye hath not seen, nor ear heard, neither have entered into the heart of man, the things which God hath prepared for them that love Him." 1 Corinthians 2:9.

The poet and the naturalist have many things to say about nature, but it is the Christian who enjoys the beauty of the earth with the highest appreciation, because he recognizes his Father's handiwork, and perceives His love in flower and shrub and tree. No one can fully appreciate the significance of hill and vale, river and sea, who does not look upon them as an expression of God's love to man.

God speaks to us through His providential workings, and through the influence of His Spirit upon the heart. In our circumstances and surroundings, in the changes daily taking place around us, we may find precious lessons, if our hearts are but open to discern them. The psalmist, tracing the work of God's providence, says, "The earth is full of the goodness of the Lord." Psalm 33:5. "Whoso is wise, and will observe these things, even they shall understand the loving-kindness of the Lord." Psalm 107:43.

God speaks to us in His Word. Here we have in clearer lines the revelation of His character, of His dealings with men, and the great work of redemption. Here is open before us the history of patriarchs and prophets and other holy men of old. They were men "subject to like passions as we are." James 5:17. We see how they struggled through discouragements like our own, how they fell under temptation as we have done, and yet took heart again and conquered through the grace of God: and, beholding, we are encouraged in our striving after righteousness. As we read of the precious experiences granted them, of the light and love and blessing it was theirs to enjoy, and of the work they wrought through the grace given them, the spirit that inspired them kindles a flame of holy emulation in our hearts, and a desire to be like them in character—like them to walk with God.

Jesus said of the Old Testament Scriptures—and how much more is it true of the New—"They are they which testify of Me" (John 5:39), the Redeemer, Him in whom our hopes of eternal life are centered. Yes, the whole Bible tells of Christ. From the first record of creation—for "without Him was not anything made that was made" (John 1:3)—to the closing promise, "Behold, I come quickly" (Revelation 22:12), we are reading of His works and listening to His voice. If you would become acquainted with the Saviour, study the Holy Scriptures.

Fill the whole heart with the words of God. They are the living water, quenching your burning thirst. They are the living bread from heaven. Jesus declares, "Except ye eat the flesh of the Son of man, and drink His blood, ye have no life in you." And He explains Himself by saying, "The words that I speak unto you, they are spirit, and they are life." John 6:53, 63. Our bodies are built up from what we eat and drink; and as in the natural economy, so in the spiritual economy: it is what we meditate upon that will give tone and strength to our spiritual nature.

The theme of redemption is one that the angels desire to look into; it will be the science and the song of the redeemed throughout the ceaseless ages of eternity. Is it not worthy of careful thought and study now? The infinite mercy and love of Jesus, the sacrifice made in our behalf, call for the most serious and solemn reflection. We should dwell upon the character of our dear Redeemer and Intercessor. We should meditate upon the mission of Him who came to save His people from their sins. As we thus contemplate heavenly themes, our faith and love will grow stronger, and our prayers will be more and more acceptable to God, because they will be more and more mixed with faith and love. They will be intelligent and fervent. There will be more constant confidence in Jesus, and a daily, living experience in His power to save to the uttermost all that come unto God by Him.

As we meditate upon the perfections of the Saviour, we shall desire to be wholly transformed, and renewed in the image of His purity. There will be a hungering and thirsting of soul to become like Him whom we adore. The more our thoughts are upon Christ, the more we shall speak of Him to others, and represent Him to the world.

The Bible was not written for the scholar alone; on the contrary, it was designed for the common people. The great truths necessary for salvation are made as clear as noonday; and none will mistake and lose their way except those who follow their own judgment instead of the plainly revealed will of God.

We should not take the testimony of any man as to what the Scriptures teach, but should study the words of God for ourselves. If we allow others to do our thinking, we shall have crippled energies and contracted abilities.

The noble powers of the mind may be so dwarfed by lack of exercise on themes worthy of their concentration as to lose their ability to grasp the deep meaning of the Word of God. The mind will enlarge if it is employed in tracing out the relation of the subjects of the Bible, comparing scripture with scripture, and spiritual things with spiritual.

There is nothing more calculated to strengthen the intellect than the study of the Scriptures. No other book is so potent to elevate the thoughts, to give vigor to the faculties, as the broad, ennobling truths of the Bible. If God's Word were studied as it should be, men would have a breadth of mind, a nobility of character, and a stability of purpose rarely seen in these times.

But there is but little benefit derived from a hasty reading of the Scriptures. One may read the whole Bible through, and yet fail to see its beauty or comprehend its deep and hidden meaning. One passage studied until its significance is clear to the mind, and its relation to the plan of salvation is evident, is of more value than the perusal of many chapters with no definite purpose in view and no positive instruction gained. Keep your Bible with you. As you have opportunity, read it; fix the texts in your memory. Even while you are walking the streets, you may read a passage, and meditate upon it, thus fixing it in the mind.

We cannot obtain wisdom without earnest attention and prayerful study. Some portions of Scripture are indeed too plain to be misunderstood; but there are others whose meaning does not lie on the surface, to be seen at a glance. Scripture must be compared with scripture. There must be careful research and prayerful reflection. And such study will be richly repaid. As the miner discovers veins of precious metal concealed beneath the surface of the earth, so will he who perseveringly searches the Word of God as for hid treasure, find truths of the greatest value, which are concealed from the view of the careless seeker. The words of inspiration, pondered in the heart, will be as streams flowing from the fountain of life.

Never should the Bible be studied without prayer. Before opening its pages we should ask for the enlightenment of the Holy Spirit, and it will be given. When Nathanael came to Jesus, the Saviour exclaimed, "Behold an Israelite indeed, in whom is no guile!" Nathanael said, "Whence knowest Thou me?" Jesus answered, "Before that Philip called thee, when thou wast under the fig tree, I saw thee." John 1:47, 48. And Jesus will see us also in the secret places of prayer, if we will seek Him for light that we may know what is truth. Angels from the world of light will be with those who in humility of heart seek for divine guidance.

The Holy Spirit exalts and glorifies the Saviour. It is His office to present Christ, the purity of His righteousness, and the great salvation that we have through Him. Jesus says, "He shall receive of Mine, and shall show it unto you." John 16:14. The Spirit of truth is the only effectual teacher of divine truth. How must God esteem the human race, since He gave His Son to die for them, and appoints His Spirit to be man's teacher and continual guide!

CHAPTER 11

HIDDEN TREASURE

THROUGH NATURE AND revelation, through His providence, and by the influence of His Spirit, God speaks to us. But these are not enough; we need also to pour out our hearts to Him. In order to have spiritual life and energy, we must have actual communion with our heavenly Father. Our minds may be drawn out toward Him; we may meditate upon His works, His mercies, His blessings; but this is not, in the fullest sense, communing with Him. In order to commune with God, we must have something to say to Him concerning our actual life.

Prayer is the opening of the heart to God as to a friend. Not that it is necessary, in order to make known to God what we are, but in order to enable us to receive Him. Prayer does not bring God down to us, but brings us up to Him.

When Jesus was upon the earth, He taught His disciples how to pray. He directed them to present their daily needs before God, and to cast all their care upon Him. And the assurance He gave them that their petitions should be heard, is assurance also to us.

Jesus Himself, while He dwelt among men, was often in prayer. Our Saviour identified Himself with our needs and weakness, in that He became a suppliant, a petitioner, seeking from His Father fresh supplies of strength, that He might come forth braced for duty and trial. He is our example in all things. He is a brother in our infirmities, "in all points tempted like as we are;" but as the Sinless One His nature recoiled from evil; He endured struggles and torture of soul in a world of sin. His humanity made prayer a necessity and a privilege. He found comfort and joy in communion with His Father. And if the Saviour of men, the Son of God, felt the need of prayer, how much more should feeble, sinful mortals feel the necessity of fervent, constant prayer.

Our heavenly Father waits to bestow upon us the fullness of His blessing. It is our privilege to drink largely at the fountain of boundless love. What a wonder it is that we pray so little! God is ready and willing to hear the sincere prayer of the humblest of His children, and yet there is much manifest reluctance on our part to make known our wants to God. What can the angels of heaven think of poor helpless human beings, who are subject to temptation, when God's heart of infinite love yearns toward them, ready to give them more than they can ask or think, and yet they pray so little, and have so little faith? The angels love to bow before God; they love to be near Him. They regard communion with God as their highest joy; and yet the children of earth, who need so much the help that God only can give, seem satisfied to walk without the light of His Spirit, the companionship of His presence.

The darkness of the evil one encloses those who neglect to pray. The whispered temptations of the enemy entice them to sin; and it is all because they do not make use of the privileges that God has given them in the divine appointment of prayer. Why should the sons and daughters of God be reluctant to pray, when prayer is the key in the hand of faith to unlock heaven's storehouse, where are treasured the boundless resources of Omnipotence? Without unceasing prayer and diligent watching, we are in danger of growing careless and of deviating from the right path. The adversary seeks continually to obstruct the way to the mercy seat, that we may not by earnest supplication and faith obtain grace and power to resist temptation.

There are certain conditions upon which we may expect that God will hear and answer our prayers. One of the first of these is that we feel our need of help from Him. He has promised, "I will pour water upon him that

is thirsty, and floods upon the dry ground." Isaiah 44:3.
Those who hunger and thirst after righteousness, who
long after God, may be sure that they will be filled. The
heart must be open to the Spirit's influence, or God's
blessing cannot be received.

Our great need is itself an argument, and pleads most
eloquently in our behalf. But the Lord is to be sought
unto to do these things for us. He says, "Ask, and it shall
be given you." And "He that spared not His own Son,
but delivered Him up for us all, how shall He not with
Him also freely give us all things?" Matthew 7:7;
Romans 8:32.

If we regard iniquity in our hearts, if we cling to any
known sin, the Lord will not hear us; but the prayer of the
penitent, contrite soul is always accepted. When all
known wrongs are righted, we may believe that God will
answer our petitions. Our own merit will never commend
us to the favor of God; it is the worthiness of Jesus that
will save us, His blood that will cleanse us; yet we have a
work to do in complying with the conditions of
acceptance.

Another element of prevailing prayer is faith. "He
that cometh to God must believe that He is, and that He is
a rewarder of them that diligently seek Him." Hebrews
11:6. Jesus said to His disciples, "What things soever ye
desire, when ye pray, believe that ye receive them, and ye
shall have them." Mark 11:24. Do we take Him at His
word?

The assurance is broad and unlimited, and He is
faithful who has promised. When we do not receive the
very things we ask for, at the time we ask, we are still to
believe that the Lord hears, and that He will answer our
prayers. We are so erring and shortsighted that we
sometimes ask for things that would not be a blessing to
us, and our heavenly Father in love answers our prayers
by giving us that which will be for our highest good—
that which we ourselves would desire if with vision
divinely enlightened we could see all things as they really
are. When our prayers seem not to be answered, we are to

cling to the promise; for the time of answering will surely
come, and we shall receive the blessing we need most.
But to claim that prayer will always be answered in the
very way and for the particular thing that we desire, is
presumption. God is too wise to err, and too good to
withhold any good thing from them that walk uprightly.
Then do not fear to trust Him, even though you do not see
the immediate answer to your prayers. Rely upon His
sure promise, "Ask, and it shall be given you." Matthew
7:7.

If we take counsel with our doubts and fears, or try to
solve everything that we cannot see clearly, before we
have faith, perplexities will only increase and deepen. But
if we come to God, feeling helpless and dependent, as we
really are, and in humble, trusting faith make known our
wants to Him whose knowledge is infinite, who sees
everything in creation, and who governs everything by
His will and word, He can and will attend to our cry, and
will let light shine into our hearts. Through sincere
prayer we are brought into connection with the mind of
the Infinite. We may have no remarkable evidence at the
time that the face of our Redeemer is bending over us in
compassion and love; but this is even so. We may not
feel His visible touch, but His hand is upon us in love
and pitying tenderness.

When we come to ask mercy and blessing from God,
we should have a spirit of love and forgiveness in our own
hearts. How can we pray, "Forgive us our debts, *as* we
forgive our debtors" (Matthew 6:12), and yet indulge an
unforgiving spirit? If we expect our own prayers to be
heard, we must forgive others in the same manner, and to
the same extent, as we hope to be forgiven.

Perseverance in prayer has been made a condition of
receiving. We must pray always, if we would grow in
faith and experience. We are to be "instant in prayer," to
"continue in prayer, and watch in the same with
thanksgiving." Romans 12:12; Colossians 4:2. Peter
exhorts believers to be "sober, and watch unto prayer." 1
Peter 4:7. Paul directs, "In everything by prayer and

supplication with thanksgiving let your requests be made known unto God." Philippians 4:6. "But ye, beloved," says Jude, "praying in the Holy Ghost, keep yourselves in the love of God." Jude 20, 21. Unceasing prayer is the unbroken union of the soul with God, so that life from God flows into our life; and from our life, purity and holiness flow back to God.

There is necessity for diligence in prayer; let nothing hinder you. Make every effort to keep open the communion between Jesus and your own soul. Seek every opportunity to go where prayer is wont to be made. Those who are really seeking for communion with God, will be seen in the prayer meeting, faithful to do their duty, and earnest and anxious to reap all the benefits they can gain. They will improve every opportunity of placing themselves where they can receive the rays of light from heaven.

We should pray in the family circle; and above all we must not neglect secret prayer; for this is the life of the soul. It is impossible for the soul to flourish while prayer is neglected. Family or public prayer alone is not sufficient. In solitude let the soul be laid open to the inspecting eye of God. Secret prayer is to be heard only by the prayer-hearing God. No curious ear is to receive the burden of such petitions. In secret prayer the soul is free from surrounding influences, free from excitement. Calmly, yet fervently, will it reach out after God. Sweet and abiding will be the influence emanating from Him who seeth in secret, whose ear is open to hear the prayer arising from the heart. By calm, simple faith, the soul holds communion with God, and gathers to itself rays of divine light to strengthen and sustain it in the conflict with Satan. God is our tower of strength.

Pray in your closet; and as you go about your daily labor, let your heart be often uplifted to God. It was thus that Enoch walked with God. These silent prayers rise like precious incense before the throne of grace. Satan cannot overcome him whose heart is thus stayed upon God.

There is no time or place in which it is inappropriate to offer up a petition to God. There is nothing that can prevent us from lifting up our hearts in the spirit of earnest prayer. In the crowds of the street, in the midst of a business engagement, we may send up a petition to God, and plead for divine guidance, as did Nehemiah when he made his request before King Artaxerxes. A closet of communion may be found wherever we are. We should have the door of the heart open continually, and our invitation going up that Jesus may come and abide as a heavenly guest in the soul.

Although there may be a tainted, corrupted atmosphere around us, we need not breathe its miasma, but may live in the pure air of heaven. We may close every door to impure imaginings and unholy thoughts by lifting the soul into the presence of God through sincere prayer. Those whose hearts are open to receive the support and blessing of God will walk in a holier atmosphere than that of earth, and will have constant communion with heaven.

We need to have more distinct views of Jesus, and a fuller comprehension of the value of eternal realities. The beauty of holiness is to fill the hearts of God's children; and that this may be accomplished, we should seek for divine disclosures of heavenly things.

Let the soul be drawn out and upward, that God may grant us a breath of the heavenly atmosphere. We may keep so near to God that in every unexpected trial our thoughts will turn to Him as naturally as the flower turns to the sun.

Keep your wants, your joys, your sorrows, your cares, and your fears, before God. You cannot burden Him; you cannot weary Him. He who numbers the hairs of your head is not indifferent to the wants of His children. "The Lord is very pitiful, and of tender mercy." James 5:11. His heart of love is touched by our sorrows, and even by our utterance of them. Take to Him everything that perplexes the mind. Nothing is too great for Him to bear, for He holds up worlds, He rules over all the affairs of the universe. Nothing that in any way concerns our peace is too small for Him to notice. There is no chapter in our experience too dark for Him to read; there is no perplexity too difficult for Him to unravel. No calamity can befall the least of His children, no anxiety harass the soul, no joy cheer, no sincere prayer escape the lips, of which our heavenly Father is unobservant, or in which He takes no immediate interest. "He healeth the broken in heart, and bindeth up their wounds." Psalm 147:3. The relations between God and each soul are as distinct and full as though there were not another soul upon the earth to share His watchcare, not another soul for whom He gave His beloved Son.

Jesus said, "Ye shall ask in My name: and I say not unto you, that I will pray the Father for you: for the Father Himself loveth you." "I have chosen you, . . . that whatsoever ye shall ask of the Father in My name, He may give it you." John 16:26, 27; 15:16. But to pray in the name of Jesus is something more than a mere mention of that name at the beginning and the ending of a prayer. It is to pray in the mind and spirit of Jesus, while we believe His promises, rely upon His grace and work His works.

God does not mean that any of us should become hermits or monks, and retire from the world, in order to devote ourselves to acts of worship. The life must be like Christ's life—between the mountain and the multitude. He who does nothing but pray will soon cease to pray, or his prayers will become a formal routine. When men take themselves out of social life, away from the sphere of Christian duty and crossbearing; when they cease to work earnestly for the Master, who worked earnestly for them, they lose the subject matter of prayer, and have no incentive to devotion. Their prayers become personal and selfish. They cannot pray in regard to the wants of humanity or the upbuilding of Christ's kingdom, pleading for strength wherewith to work.

We sustain a loss when we neglect the privilege of associating together to strengthen and encourage one another in the service of God. The truths of His Word lose their vividness and importance in our minds. Our hearts cease to be enlightened and aroused by their sanctifying influence, and we decline in spirituality. In our association as Christians we lose much by lack of sympathy with one another. He who shuts himself up to himself is not filling the position that God designed he should. The proper cultivation of the social elements in our nature brings us into sympathy with others, and is a means of development and strength to us in the service of God.

If Christians would associate together, speaking to each other of the love of God, and of the precious truths of redemption, their own hearts would be refreshed, and they would refresh one another. We may be daily learning more of our heavenly Father, gaining a fresh experience of His grace; then we shall desire to speak of His love; and as we do this, our own hearts will be warmed and encouraged. If we thought and talked more of Jesus, and less of self, we should have far more of His presence.

If we would but think of God as often as we have evidence of His care for us, we should keep Him ever in our thoughts, and should delight to talk of Him and to praise Him. We talk of temporal things because we have an interest in them. We talk of our friends because we love them; our joys and our sorrows are bound up with them. Yet we have infinitely greater reason to love God than to love our earthly friends; it should be the most natural thing in the world to make Him first in all our thoughts, to talk of His goodness and tell of His power. The rich gifts He has bestowed upon us were not intended to absorb our thoughts and love so much that we should have nothing to give to God; they are constantly to remind us of Him, and to bind us in bonds of love and gratitude to our heavenly Benefactor. We dwell too near the lowlands of earth. Let us raise our eyes to the open door of the sanctuary above, where the light of the glory of God shines in the face of Christ, who "is able also to save them to the uttermost that come unto God by Him."

Hebrews 7:25.

We need to praise God more "for His goodness, and for His wonderful works to the children of men." Psalm 107:8. Our devotional exercises should not consist wholly in asking and receiving. Let us not be always thinking of our wants, and never of the benefits we receive. We do not pray any too much, but we are too sparing of giving thanks. We are the constant recipients of God's mercies, and yet how little gratitude we express, how little we praise Him for what He has done for us.

Anciently the Lord bade Israel, when they met together for His service, "Ye shall eat before the Lord your God, and ye shall rejoice in all that ye put your hand unto, ye and your households, wherein the Lord thy God hath blessed thee." Deuteronomy 12:7. That which is done for the glory of God should be done with cheerfulness, with songs of praise and thanksgiving, not with sadness and gloom.

Our God is a tender, merciful Father. His service should not be looked upon as a heart-saddening, distressing exercise. It should be a pleasure to worship the Lord and to take part in His work. God would not have His children, for whom so great salvation has been provided, act as if He were a hard, exacting taskmaster. He is their best friend; and when they worship Him, He expects to be with them, to bless and comfort them, filling their hearts with joy and love. The Lord desires His children to take comfort in His service, and to find more pleasure than hardship in His work. He desires that those who come to worship Him shall carry away with them precious thoughts of His care and love, that they may be cheered in all the employments of daily life, that they may have grace to deal honestly and faithfully in all things.

We must gather about the cross. Christ and Him crucified should be the theme of contemplation, of conversation, and of our most joyful emotion. We should keep in our thoughts every blessing we receive from God, and when we realize His great love, we should be willing to trust everything to the hand that was nailed to the cross for us.

The soul may ascend nearer heaven on the wings of praise. God is worshiped with song and music in the courts above, and as we express our gratitude, we are approximating to the worship of the heavenly hosts. "Whoso offereth praise glorifieth" God. Psalm 50:23. Let us with reverent joy come before our Creator, with "thanksgiving, and the voice of melody." Isaiah 51:3.

CHAPTER 12

OVERCOMING DOUBT

MANY, ESPECIALLY THOSE who are young in the Christian life, are at times troubled with the suggestions of skepticism. There are in the Bible many things which they cannot explain, or even understand, and Satan employs these to shake their faith in the Scriptures as a revelation from God. They ask, "How shall I know the right way? If the Bible is indeed the Word of God, how can I be freed from these doubts and perplexities?"

God never asks us to believe, without giving sufficient evidence upon which to base our faith. His existence, His character, the truthfulness of His Word, are all established by testimony that appeals to our reason; and this testimony is abundant. Yet God has never removed the possibility of doubt. Our faith must rest upon evidence, not demonstration. Those who wish to doubt will have opportunity; while those who really desire to know the truth, will find plenty of evidence on which to rest their faith.

It is impossible for finite minds fully to comprehend the character or the works of the Infinite One. To the keenest intellect, the most highly educated mind, that holy Being must ever remain clothed in mystery. "Canst thou by searching find out God? canst thou find out the Almighty unto perfection? It is as high as heaven; what canst thou do? deeper than hell; what canst thou know?" Job 11:7, 8.

The apostle Paul exclaims, "O the depth of the riches both of the wisdom and knowledge of God! how unsearchable are His judgments, and His ways past finding out!" Romans 11:33. But though "clouds and darkness are round about Him," "righteousness and judgment are the foundation of His throne." Psalm 97:2, R.V. We can so far comprehend His dealings with us, and the motives by which He is actuated, that we may discern boundless love and mercy united to infinite power. We can understand as much of His purposes as it is for our good to know; and beyond this we must still trust the hand that is omnipotent, the heart that is full of love.

The Word of God, like the character of its divine Author, presents mysteries that can never be fully comprehended by finite beings. The entrance of sin into the world, the incarnation of Christ, regeneration, the resurrection, and many other subjects presented in the Bible, are mysteries too deep for the human mind to explain, or even fully to comprehend. But we have no reason to doubt God's Word because we cannot understand the mysteries of His providence. In the natural world we are constantly surrounded with mysteries that we cannot fathom. The very humblest forms of life present a problem that the wisest of philosophers is powerless to explain. Everywhere are wonders beyond our ken. Should we then be surprised to find that in the spiritual world also there are mysteries that we cannot fathom? The difficulty lies solely in the weakness and narrowness of the human mind. God has given us in the Scriptures sufficient evidence of their divine character, and we are not to doubt His Word because we cannot understand all the mysteries of His providence.

The apostle Peter says that there are in Scripture "things hard to be understood, which they that are unlearned and unstable wrest . . . unto their own destruction." 2 Peter 3:16. The difficulties of Scripture have been urged by skeptics as an argument against the Bible; but so far from this, they constitute a strong evidence of its divine inspiration. If it contained no account of God but that which we could easily comprehend; if His greatness and majesty could be grasped by finite minds, then the Bible would not bear the unmistakable credentials of divine authority. The very grandeur and mystery of the themes presented, should inspire faith in it as the Word of God.

The Bible unfolds truth with a simplicity and a perfect adaptation to the needs and longings of the human heart, that has astonished and charmed the most highly cultivated minds, while it enables the humblest and uncultured to discern the way of salvation. And yet these simply stated truths lay hold upon subjects so elevated, so far-reaching, so infinitely beyond the power of human comprehension, that we can accept them only because God has declared them. Thus the plan of redemption is laid open to us, so that every soul may see the steps he is to take in repentance toward God, and faith toward our Lord Jesus Christ, in order to be saved in God's appointed way; yet beneath these truths, so easily understood, lie mysteries that are the hiding of His glory—mysteries that overpower the mind in its research, yet inspire the sincere seeker for truth with reverence and faith. The more he searches the Bible, the deeper is his conviction that it is the word of the living God, and human reason bows before the majesty of divine revelation.

To acknowledge that we cannot fully comprehend the great truths of the Bible is only to admit that the finite mind is inadequate to grasp the infinite; that man, with his limited, human knowledge, cannot understand the purposes of Omniscience.

Because they cannot fathom all its mysteries, the skeptic and the infidel reject God's Word; and not all who profess to believe the Bible are free from danger on this point. The apostle says, "Take heed, brethren, lest there be in any of you an evil heart of unbelief, in departing from the living God." Hebrews 3:12. It is right to study closely the teachings of the Bible, and to search into "the deep things of God" (1 Corinthians 2:10), so far as they are revealed in Scripture. While "the secret things belong unto the Lord our God," "those things which are revealed belong unto us." Deuteronomy 29:29. But it is Satan's work to pervert the investigative powers of the mind. A certain pride is mingled with the consideration of Bible truth, so that men feel impatient and defeated if they cannot explain every portion of Scripture to their satisfaction. It is too humiliating to them to acknowledge that they do not understand the inspired words. They are unwilling to wait patiently until God shall see fit to reveal the truth to them. They feel that their unaided human wisdom is sufficient to enable them to comprehend the Scripture, and failing to do this, they virtually deny its authority. It is true that many theories and doctrines popularly supposed to be derived from the Bible have no foundation in its teaching, and indeed are contrary to the whole tenor of inspiration. These things have been a cause of doubt and perplexity to many minds. They are not, however, chargeable to God's Word, but to man's perversion of it.

If it were possible for created beings to attain to a full understanding of God and His works, then, having reached this point, there would be for them no further discovery of truth, no growth in knowledge, no further development of mind or heart. God would no longer be supreme; and man, having reached the limit of knowledge and attainment, would cease to advance. Let us thank God that it is not so. God is infinite; in Him are "all the treasures of wisdom and knowledge." Colossians 2:3. And to all eternity men may be ever searching, ever learning, and yet never exhaust the treasures of His wisdom, His goodness, and His power.

God intends that even in this life the truths of His Word shall be ever unfolding to His people. There is only one way in which this knowledge can be obtained. We can attain to an understanding of God's Word only through the illumination of that Spirit by which the Word was given. "The things of God knoweth no man, but the Spirit of God;" "for the Spirit searcheth all things, yea the deep things of God." 1 Corinthians 2:11, 10. And the Saviour's promise to His followers was, "When He, the Spirit of truth, is come, He will guide you into all truth.... For He shall receive of Mine, and shall show it unto you." John 16:13, 14.

God desires man to exercise his reasoning powers; and

the study of the Bible will strengthen and elevate the mind as no other study can. Yet we are to beware of deifying reason, which is subject to the weakness and infirmity of humanity. If we would not have the Scriptures clouded to our understanding, so that the plainest truths shall not be comprehended, we must have the simplicity and faith of a little child, ready to learn, and beseeching the aid of the Holy Spirit. A sense of the power and wisdom of God, and of our inability to comprehend His greatness, should inspire us with humility, and we should open His Word, as we would enter His presence, with holy awe. When we come to the Bible, reason must acknowledge an authority superior to itself, and heart and intellect must bow to the great I AM.

There are many things apparently difficult or obscure, which God will make plain and simple to those who thus seek an understanding of them. But without the guidance of the Holy Spirit we shall be continually liable to wrest the Scriptures or to misinterpret them. There is much reading of the Bible that is without profit, and in many cases a positive injury. When the Word of God is opened without reverence and without prayer; when the thoughts and affections are not fixed upon God, or in harmony with His will, the mind is clouded with doubt; and in the very study of the Bible, skepticism strengthens. The enemy takes control of the thoughts, and he suggests interpretations that are not correct. Whenever men are not in word and deed seeking to be in harmony with God, then, however learned they may be, they are liable to err in their understanding of Scripture, and it is not safe to trust to their explanations. Those who look to the Scriptures to find discrepancies, have not spiritual insight. With distorted vision they will see many causes for doubt and unbelief in things that are really plain and simple.

Disguise it as they may, the real cause of doubt and skepticism, in most cases, is the love of sin. The teachings and restrictions of God's Word are not welcome to the proud, sin-loving heart, and those who are unwilling to obey its requirements are ready to doubt its authority. In order to arrive at truth, we must have a sincere desire to know the truth, and a willingness of heart to obey it. And all who come in this spirit to the study of the Bible, will find abundant evidence that it is God's Word, and they may gain an understanding of its truths that will make them wise unto salvation.

Christ has said, "If any man willeth to do His will, he shall know of the teaching." John 7:17, R.V. Instead of questioning and caviling concerning that which you do not understand, give heed to the light that already shines upon you, and you will receive greater light. By the grace of Christ, perform every duty that has been made plain to your understanding, and you will be enabled to understand and perform those of which you are now in doubt.

There is an evidence that is open to all—the most highly educated, and the most illiterate—the evidence of experience. God invites us to prove for ourselves the reality of His Word, the truth of His promises. He bids us "taste and see that the Lord is good." Psalm 34:8. Instead of depending upon the word of another, we are to taste for ourselves. He declares, "Ask, and ye shall receive." John 16:24. His promises will be fulfilled. They have never failed; they never can fail. And as we draw near to Jesus, and rejoice in the fullness of His love, our doubt and darkness will disappear in the light of His presence.

The apostle Paul says that God "hath delivered us from the power of darkness, and hath translated us into the kingdom of His dear Son." Colossians 1:13. And every one who has passed from death unto life is able to "set to his seal that God is true." John 3:33. He can testify, "I needed help, and I found it in Jesus. Every want was supplied, the hunger of my soul was satisfied; and now the Bible is to me the revelation of Jesus Christ. Do you ask why I believe in Jesus? Because He is to me a divine Saviour. Why do I believe the Bible? Because I have found it to be the voice of God to my soul." We may have the witness in ourselves that the Bible is true, that Christ is the Son of God. We know that we are not following cunningly devised fables.

Peter exhorts his brethren to "grow in grace, and in the knowledge of our Lord and Saviour Jesus Christ." 2 Peter 3:18. When the people of God are growing in grace, they will be constantly obtaining a clearer understanding of His Word. They will discern new light and beauty in its sacred truths. This has been true in the history of the church in all ages, and thus it will continue to the end. "The path of the righteous is as the light of dawn, that shineth more and more unto the perfect day." Proverbs 4:18, R.V., margin.

By faith we may look to the hereafter, and grasp the pledge of God for a growth of intellect, the human faculties uniting with the divine, and every power of the soul being brought into direct contact with the Source of light. We may rejoice that all which has perplexed us in the providences of God will then be made plain, things hard to be understood will then find an explanation; and where our finite minds discovered only confusion and broken purposes, we shall see the most perfect and beautiful harmony. "Now we see through a glass, darkly; but then face to face: now I know in part; but then shall I know even as also I am known." 1 Corinthians 13:12.

CHAPTER 13

REJOICING WITHIN

THE CHILDREN OF GOD are called to be representatives of Christ, showing forth the goodness and mercy of the Lord. As Jesus has revealed to us the true character of the Father, so we are to reveal Christ to a world that does not know His tender, pitying love. "As Thou has sent Me into the world," said Jesus, "even so have I also sent them into the world." "I in them, and Thou in Me, . . . that the world may know that Thou hast sent Me." John 17:18, 23. The apostle Paul says to the disciples of Jesus, "Ye are manifestly declared to be the epistle of Christ," "known and read of all men." 2 Corinthians 3:3, 2. In every one of His children, Jesus sends a letter to the world. If you are Christ's follower, He sends in you a letter to the family, the village, the street, where you live. Jesus, dwelling in you, desires to speak to the hearts of those who are not acquainted with Him. Perhaps they do not read the Bible, or do not hear the voice that speaks to them in its pages; they do not see the love of God through His works. But if you are a true representative of Jesus, it may be that through you they will be led to understand something of His goodness, and be won to love and serve Him.

Christians are set as light bearers on the way to heaven. They are to reflect to the world the light shining upon them from Christ. Their life and character should be such that through them others will get a right conception of Christ and of His service.

If we do represent Christ, we shall make His service appear attractive, as it really is. Christians who gather up gloom and sadness to their souls, and murmur and complain, are giving to others a false representation of God and the Christian life. They give the impression that

God is not pleased to have His children happy, and in this they bear false witness against our heavenly Father.

Satan is exultant when he can lead the children of God into unbelief and despondency. He delights to see us mistrusting God, doubting His willingness and power to save us. He loves to have us feel that the Lord will do us harm by His providences. It is the work of Satan to represent the Lord as lacking in compassion and pity. He misstates the truth in regard to Him. He fills the imagination with false ideas concerning God; and instead of dwelling upon the truth in regard to our heavenly Father, we too often fix our minds upon the misrepresentations of Satan, and dishonor God by distrusting Him and murmuring against Him. Satan ever seeks to make the religious life one of gloom. He desires it to appear toilsome and difficult; and when the Christian presents in his own life this view of religion, he is, through his unbelief, seconding the falsehood of Satan.

Many, walking along the path of life, dwell upon their mistakes and failures and disappointments, and their hearts are filled with grief and discouragement. While I was in Europe, a sister who had been doing this, and who was in deep distress, wrote to me, asking for some word of encouragement. The night after I had read her letter, I dreamed that I was in a garden, and one who seemed to be the owner of the garden was conducting me through its paths. I was gathering the flowers and enjoying their fragrance, when this sister, who had been walking by my side, called my attention to some unsightly briers that were impeding her way. There she was mourning and grieving. She was not walking in the pathway, following the guide, but was walking among the briers and thorns. "Oh," she mourned, "is it not a pity that this beautiful garden is spoiled with thorns?" Then the guide said, "Let the thorns alone, for they will only wound you. Gather the roses, the lilies, and the pinks."

Have there not been some bright spots in your experience? Have you not had some precious seasons when your heart throbbed with joy in response to the

Spirit of God? When you look back into the chapters of your life experience, do you not find some pleasant pages? Are not God's promises, like the fragrant flowers, growing beside your path on every hand? Will you not let their beauty and sweetness fill your heart with joy?

The briers and thorns will only wound and grieve you; and if you gather only these things, and present them to others, are you not, besides slighting the goodness of God yourself, preventing those around you from walking in the path of life?

It is not wise to gather together all the unpleasant recollections of a past life—its iniquities and disappointments—to talk over them and mourn over them until we are overwhelmed with discouragement. A discouraged soul is filled with darkness, shutting out the light of God from his own soul, and casting a shadow upon the pathway of others.

Thank God for the bright pictures which He has presented to us. Let us group together the blessed assurances of His love, that we may look upon them continually: The Son of God leaving His Father's throne, clothing His divinity with humanity, that He might rescue man from the power of Satan; His triumph in our behalf, opening heaven to men, revealing to human vision the presence chamber where the Deity unveils His glory; the fallen race uplifted from the pit of ruin into which sin had plunged it, and brought again into connection with the infinite God, and having endured the divine test through faith in our Redeemer, clothed in the righteousness of Christ, and exalted to His throne—these are the pictures which God would have us contemplate.

When we seem to doubt God's love, and distrust His promises, we dishonor Him and grieve His Holy Spirit. How would a mother feel if her children were constantly complaining of her, just as though she did not mean them well, when her whole life's effort had been to forward their interests and to give them comfort? Suppose they should doubt her love; it would break her heart. How would any parent feel to be thus treated by his children? And how can our heavenly Father regard us when we distrust His love, which has led Him to give His only begotten Son that we might have life? The apostle writes, "He that spared not His own Son, but delivered Him up for us all, how shall He not with Him also freely give us all things?" Romans 8:32. And yet how many, by their actions, if not in word, are saying, "The Lord does not mean this for me. Perhaps He loves others, but He does not love me."

All this is harming your own soul; for every word of doubt you utter is inviting Satan's temptations; it is strengthening in you the tendency to doubt, and it is grieving from you the ministering angels. When Satan tempts you, breathe not a word of doubt or darkness. If you choose to open the door to his suggestions, your mind will be filled with distrust and rebellious questioning. If you talk out your feelings, every doubt you express not only reacts upon yourself, but it is a seed that will germinate and bear fruit in the life of others, and it may be impossible to counteract the influence of your words. You yourself may be able to recover from the season of temptation and from the snare of Satan, but others, who have been swayed by your influence, may not be able to escape from the unbelief you have suggested. How important that we speak only those things that will give spiritual strength and life!

Angels are listening to hear what kind of report you are bearing to the world about your heavenly Master. Let your conversation be of Him who liveth to make intercession for you before the Father. When you take the hand of a friend, let praise to God be on your lips and in your heart. This will attract his thoughts to Jesus.

All have trials; griefs hard to bear, temptations hard to resist. Do not tell your troubles to your fellow mortals, but carry everything to God in prayer. Make it a rule never to utter one word of doubt or discouragement. You can do much to brighten the life of others and strengthen their efforts, by words of hope and holy cheer.

There is many a brave soul sorely pressed by

temptation, almost ready to faint in the conflict with self and with the powers of evil. Do not discourage such a one in his hard struggle. Cheer him with brave, hopeful words that shall urge him on his way. Thus the light of Christ may shine from you. "None of us liveth to himself." Romans 14:7. By our unconscious influence others may be encouraged and strengthened, or they may be discouraged, and repelled from Christ and the truth.

There are many who have an erroneous idea of the life and character of Christ. They think that He was devoid of warmth and sunniness, that He was stern, severe, and joyless. In many cases the whole religious experience is colored by these gloomy views.

It is often said that Jesus wept, but that He was never known to smile. Our Saviour was indeed a Man of Sorrows, and acquainted with grief, for He opened His heart to all the woes of men. But though His life was self-denying and shadowed with pain and care, His spirit was not crushed. His countenance did not wear an expression of grief and repining, but ever one of peaceful serenity. His heart was a wellspring of life; and wherever He went, He carried rest and peace, joy and gladness.

Our Saviour was deeply serious and intensely in earnest, but never gloomy or morose. The life of those who imitate Him will be full of earnest purpose; they will have a deep sense of personal responsibility. Levity will be repressed; there will be no boisterous merriment, no rude jesting; but the religion of Jesus gives peace like a river. It does not quench the light of joy; it does not restrain cheerfulness, nor cloud the sunny, smiling face. Christ came not to be ministered unto but to minister; and when His love reigns in the heart, we shall follow His example.

If we keep uppermost in our minds the unkind and unjust acts of others, we shall find it impossible to love them as Christ has loved us; but if our thoughts dwell upon the wondrous love and pity of Christ for us, the same spirit will flow out to others. We should love and respect one another, notwithstanding the faults and imperfections that we cannot help seeing. Humility and self-distrust should be cultivated, and a patient tenderness with the faults of others. This will kill out all narrowing selfishness, and make us largehearted and generous.

The psalmist says, "Trust in the Lord, and do good; so shalt thou dwell in the land, and verily, thou shalt be fed." Psalm 37:3. "Trust in the Lord." Each day has its burdens, its cares and perplexities; and when we meet, how ready we are to talk of our difficulties and trials. So many borrowed troubles intrude, so many fears are indulged, such a weight of anxiety is expressed, that one might suppose we had no pitying, loving Saviour, ready to hear all our requests, and to be to us a present help in every time of need.

Some are always fearing, and borrowing trouble. Every day they are surrounded with the tokens of God's love; every day they are enjoying the bounties of His providence; but they overlook these present blessings. Their minds are continually dwelling upon something disagreeable, which they fear may come; or some difficulty may really exist, which, though small, blinds their eyes to the many things that demand gratitude. The difficulties they encounter, instead of driving them to God, the only source of their help, separate them from Him, because they awaken unrest and repining.

Do we well to be thus unbelieving? Why should we be ungrateful and distrustful? Jesus is our friend; all heaven is interested in our welfare. We should not allow the perplexities and worries of everyday life to fret the mind and cloud the brow. If we do, we shall always have something to vex and annoy. We should not indulge a solicitude that only frets and wears us, but does not help us to bear trials.

You may be perplexed in business; your prospects may grow darker and darker, and you may be threatened with loss; but do not become discouraged; cast your care upon God, and remain calm and cheerful. Pray for wisdom to manage your affairs with discretion, and thus prevent loss and disaster. Do all you can on your part to bring about favorable results. Jesus has promised His aid, but not apart from our effort. When, relying upon our Helper, you have done all you can, accept the result cheerfully.

It is not the will of God that His people should be weighed down with care. But our Lord does not deceive us. He does not say to us, "Do not fear; there are no dangers in your path." He knows there are trials and dangers, and He deals with us plainly. He does not propose to take His people out of a world of sin and evil, but He points them to a never-failing refuge. His prayer for His disciples was, "I pray not that Thou shouldest take them out of the world, but that Thou shouldest keep them from the evil." "In the world," He says, "ye shall have tribulation: but be of good cheer; I have overcome the world." John 17:15; 16:33.

In His Sermon on the Mount, Christ taught His disciples precious lessons in regard to the necessity of trusting in God. These lessons were designed to encourage the children of God through all ages, and they have come down to our time full of instruction and comfort. The Saviour pointed His followers to the birds of the air as they warbled their carols of praise, unencumbered with thoughts of care, for "they sow not, neither do they reap." And yet the great Father provides for their needs. The Saviour asks, "Are ye not much better than they?" Matthew 6:26. The great Provider for man and beast opens His hand and supplies all His creatures. The birds of the air are not beneath His notice. He does not drop the food into their bills, but He makes provision for their needs. They must gather the grains He has scattered for them. They must prepare the material for their little nests. They must feed their young. They go forth singing to their labor, for "your heavenly Father feedeth them." And "are ye not much better than they?" Are not you, as intelligent, spiritual worshipers, of more value than the birds of the air? Will not the Author of our being, the Preserver of our life, the One who formed us in His own divine image, provide for our necessities if we but trust in Him?

Christ pointed His disciples to the flowers of the field, growing in rich profusion, and glowing in the simple beauty which the heavenly Father had given them, as an expression of His love to man. He said, "Consider the lilies of the field, how they grow." The beauty and simplicity of these natural flowers far outrival the splendor of Solomon. The most gorgeous attire produced by the skill of art cannot bear comparison with the natural grace and radiant beauty of the flowers of God's creation. Jesus asks, "If God so clothe the grass of the field, which today is, and tomorrow is cast into the oven, shall He not much more clothe you, O ye of little faith?" Matthew 6:28, 30. If God, the divine Artist, gives to the simple flowers that perish in a day their delicate and varied colors, how much greater care will He have for those who are created in His own image? This lesson of Christ's is a rebuke to the anxious thought, the perplexity and doubt, of the faithless heart.

The Lord would have all His sons and daughters happy, peaceful, and obedient. Jesus says, "My peace I give unto you: not as the world giveth, give I unto you. Let not your heart be troubled, neither let it be afraid." "These things have I spoken unto you, that My joy might remain in you, and that your joy might be full." John 14:27; 15:11.

Happiness that is sought from selfish motives, outside of the path of duty, is ill-balanced, fitful, and transitory; it passes away, and the soul is filled with loneliness and sorrow; but there is joy and satisfaction in the service of God; the Christian is not left to walk in uncertain paths; he is not left to vain regrets and disappointments. If we do not have the pleasures of this life, we may still be joyful in looking to the life beyond.

But even here Christians may have the joy of communion with Christ; they may have the light of His love, the perpetual comfort of His presence. Every step in life may bring us closer to Jesus, may give us a deeper experience of His love, and may bring us one step nearer to the blessed home of peace. Then let us not cast away our confidence, but have firm assurance, firmer than ever before. "Hitherto hath the Lord helped us" (1 Samuel 7:12), and He will help us to the end. Let us look to the monumental pillars, reminders of what the Lord has done to comfort us and to save us from the hand of the destroyer. Let us keep fresh in our memory all the tender mercies that God has shown us—the tears He has wiped away, the pains He has soothed, the anxieties removed, the fears dispelled, the wants supplied, the blessings bestowed—thus strengthening ourselves for all that is before us through the remainder of our pilgrimage.

We cannot but look forward to new perplexities in the coming conflict, but we may look on what is past as well as on what is to come, and say, "Hitherto hath the Lord helped us." "As thy days, so shall thy strength be." Deuteronomy 33:25. The trial will not exceed the strength that shall be given us to bear it. Then let us take up our work just where we find it, believing that whatever may come, strength proportionate to the trial will be given.

And by and by the gates of heaven will be thrown open to admit God's children, and from the lips of the King of glory the benediction will fall on their ears like richest music, "Come, ye blessed of My Father, inherit the kingdom prepared for you from the foundation of the world." Matthew 25:34.

Then the redeemed will be welcomed to the home that Jesus is preparing for them. There their companions will not be the vile of earth, liars, idolators, the impure, and unbelieving; but they will associate with those who have overcome Satan, and through divine grace have formed perfect characters. Every sinful tendency, every imperfection, that afflicts them here, has been removed by the blood of Christ, and the excellence and brightness of His glory, far exceeding the brightness of the sun, is imparted to them. And the moral beauty, the perfection of His character, shines through them, in worth far exceeding this outward splendor. They are without fault before the great white throne, sharing the dignity and the privileges of the angels.

In view of the glorious inheritance that may be his, "what shall a man give in exchange for his soul?" Matthew 16:26. He may be poor, yet he possesses in himself a wealth and dignity that the world could never bestow. The soul redeemed and cleansed from sin, with all its noble powers dedicated to the service of God, is of surpassing worth; and there is joy in heaven in the presence of God and the holy angels over one soul redeemed, a joy that is expressed in songs of holy triumph.

PART II

THE CHRISTIAN WAY

"All scripture is given by inspiration of God, and is profitable for doctrine, for reproof, for correction, for instruction in righteousness; That the man of God may be perfect, throughly furnished unto all good works."   *2 Timothy 3:16, 17*

IS THE BIBLE TRUSTWORTHY?

How much of the Bible is inspired?

"*All scripture is given by inspiration of God*, and is profitable for doctrine, for reproof, for correction, for instruction in righteousness."

2 Timothy 3:16

How does God speak to the prophets?

"For the prophecy came not in old time by the will of man: but *holy men of God spake as they were moved by the Holy Ghost.*" 2 Peter 1:21

What three parts of the Old Testament Scripture did Jesus refer to in His teachings?

"And he said unto them, 'These are the words which I spake unto you, while I was yet with you, that *all things must be fulfilled, which were written in the law of Moses, and in the prophets, and in the psalms*, concerning me.' Then opened he their understanding, that they might understand the scriptures."

Luke 24:44,45

Note: When Jesus referred to the Scriptures, He was referring to the Old Testament, since the New Testament was not yet written.

According to Jesus, to whom does the Old Testament refer?

"Search the scriptures; for in them ye think ye have eternal life: and *they are they which testify of me."*   John 5:39

"Then he said unto them, 'O fools, and slow of heart to believe all that the prophets have spoken: Ought not Christ to have suffered these things, and to enter into his glory?' And *beginning at Moses and all the prophets, he expounded unto them in all the scriptures the things concerning himself."*
                                         Luke 24:25-27

Why are the experiences of men and women recorded in the Bible?

"Now *all these things happened unto them for examples: and they are written for our admonition,* upon whom the ends of the world are come."   1 Corinthians 10:11

Why were the New Testament experiences of Jesus recorded?

"But *these are written, that ye might believe that Jesus is the Christ, the Son of God*; and that believing ye might have life through his name."   John 20:31

What can be the result of Bible study?

"And that from a child thou hast known *the holy scriptures, which are able to make thee wise unto salvation* through faith which is in Christ Jesus."
                                         2 Timothy 3:15

What are the benefits of Scripture?

"All scripture is given by inspiration of God, and is profitable for doctrine, for reproof, for correction, for instruction in righteousness: That the man of God may be perfect, thoroughly furnished unto all good works." 2 Timothy 3:16, 17

According to Jesus, where do men find truth?

"Sanctify them through thy truth: *thy word is truth.*"
John 17:17

What mistake did the Sadducees (a sect of the Jews) make concerning the Scriptures?

"Jesus answered and said unto them, *'Ye do err, not knowing the scriptures,* nor the power of God.' "
Matthew 22:29

Why can't man, in his sinful nature, understand spiritual things?

"Now we have received, not the spirit of the world, but the spirit which is of God; that we might know the things that are freely given to us of God. Which things also we speak, not in the words which man's wisdom teacheth, but which the Holy Ghost teacheth; comparing spiritual things with spiritual. But *the natural man receiveth not the things of the spirit of God*: for they are foolishness unto him: neither can he know them, *because they are spiritually discerned.*"
1 Corinthians 2:12-14

Who only can guide us into all truth?

"Howbeit *when he, the Spirit of truth, is come, he will guide you into all truth*: for he shall not speak of himself; but whatsoever he shall hear, that shall he speak: and he will show you things to come."

John 16:13

Why should we study the Bible?

"*Study to show thyself approved unto God*, a workman that needeth not to be ashamed, rightly dividing the word of truth."   2 Timothy 2:15

How often should we study and search the Bible?

"These (Christians in Berea) were more noble than those in Thessalonica, in that *they received the word with all readiness of mind, and searched the scriptures daily*, whether those things were so."

Acts 17:11

Thought Promises:

"*Thy word is a lamp* unto my feet, *and a light* unto my path."   Psalm 119:105

"Thy word have I hid in mine heart, *that I might not sin against thee*."   Psalm 119:11

WHO IS GOD?

How does the Bible introduce God?

"In the beginning God created the heaven and the earth." Genesis 1:1

How long has God been in existence?

"Before the mountains were brought forth, or ever thou hadst formed the earth and the world, *even from everlasting to everlasting, thou art God."*

Psalm 90:2

Where is God's dwelling place?

"And hearken thou to the supplication of thy servant, and of thy people Israel, when they shall pray toward this place: and *hear thou in heaven thy dwelling place*: and when thou hearest, forgive." 1 Kings 8:30

What evidence of God's existence are we able to see or perceive?

"The heavens declare the glory of God; and the firmament showeth his handiwork." Psalm 19:1

"I will praise thee; for I am fearfully and wonderfully made: *marvellous are thy works*; and that my soul knoweth right well." Psalm 139:14

"But ask now the beasts, and they shall teach thee; and the fowls of the air, and they shall tell thee: Or speak to the earth, and it shall teach thee: and the fishes of the sea shall declare unto thee. *Who knoweth not in all these that the hand of the Lord hath wrought this?"*   Job 12:7-9

How does the true God of heaven differ from the other gods man has worshiped?

"Remember the former things of old: for I am God, and there is none else; *I am God, and there is none like me, Declaring the end from the beginning, and from ancient times the things that are not yet done,* saying, My counsel shall stand, and I will do all my pleasure."   Isaiah 46:9,10

"For all the gods of the nations are idols: *but the Lord made the heavens."*   Psalm 96:5

"For thus saith the Lord that created the heavens; God himself that formed the earth and made it; he hath established it, he created it not in vain, he formed it to be inhabited: *I am the Lord; and there is none else."*
                                       Isaiah 45:18

Scripture declarations about God:

a. *"Thou art worthy, O Lord,* to receive glory and honor and power: *for thou hast created all things,* and for thy pleasure they are and were created."
                                       Revelation 4:11

b. *"Great is our God above all gods."*
                                       2 Chronicles 2:5

c. *"With God all things are possible."*
                                       Mark 10:27

d. "He healeth the broken in heart . . . *His understanding is infinite."*   Psalm 147:3-5

e. "I am the Lord, *I change not.*" Malachi 3:6

f. "He that loveth not knoweth not God; *for God is love.*" 1 John 4:8

What description did God give of Himself to Moses?

"And the Lord passed by before him, and proclaimed, *The Lord, The Lord God, merciful and gracious, longsuffering, and abundant in goodness and truth,* Keeping mercy for thousands, forgiving iniquity and transgression and sin, and that will by no means clear the guilty; visiting the iniquity of the fathers upon the children, and upon the children's children, unto the third and to the fourth generation."

Exodus 34:6, 7

What is the relationship that God wants to have with all of us?

"Behold, what manner of love the Father hath bestowed upon us, *that we should be called the sons of God.*" 1 John 3:1

"The Lord is good to all: and his tender mercies are over all his works." Psalm 145:9

"That ye may be the children of your Father which is in heaven: for he maketh his sun to rise on the evil and on the good, and sendeth rain on the just and on the unjust." Matthew 5:45

WHY IS THERE SIN AND SUFFERING?

Who was the first sinner?

"He that committeth sin is of the devil; *for the devil sinneth from the beginning.* For this purpose the Son of God was manifested, that he might destroy the works of the devil." 1 John 3:8

How did the devil (Satan) come to this world?

"And he said unto them, *I beheld Satan as lightning fall from heaven.*" Luke 10:18

What kind of being was Satan?

"*Thou art the anointed cherub that covereth*; and I have set thee so: thou wast upon the holy mountain of God; thou hast walked up and down in the midst of the stones of fire. *Thou wast perfect in thy ways from the day that thou wast created, till iniquity was found in thee.*"

Ezekiel 28:14,15

Note: The "cherub that covereth" is a description of the angel that stood next to the throne of God in heaven (Psalm 80:1). This angel was created perfect and was the most honored of all created beings, until he made himself into a devil by trying to set his own will above the will of God.

What contributed to Satan's fall and rebellion in heaven?

"Thine heart was lifted up because of thy beauty, thou hast corrupted thy wisdom *by reason of thy brightness:* I will cast thee to the ground, I will lay thee before kings, that they may behold thee."

Ezekiel 28:17

What was Lucifer's ambition?

"How art thou fallen from heaven, O Lucifer, son of the morning! how art thou cut down to the ground, which didst weaken the nations! For thou hast said in thine heart, *I will ascend into heaven, I will exalt my throne* above the stars of God: *I will sit also upon the mount* of the congregation, in the sides of the north: *I will ascend above the heights of the clouds; I will be like the most High."* Isaiah 14:12-14

Note: Lucifer was Satan's name before his fall.

What happened in heaven after Satan rebelled?

"And *there was war in heaven:* Michael and his angels fought against the dragon; and the dragon fought and his angels. And prevailed not; neither was their place found any more in heaven. And *the great dragon was cast out, that old serpent, called the Devil, and Satan,* which deceiveth the whole world: *he was cast out into the earth,* and his angels were cast out with him." Revelation 12:7-9

To whom did Satan turn with deception after he was expelled from heaven?

"Now the serpent was more subtil than any beast of the field which the Lord God had made. And *he said unto the woman,* Yea, hath God said, Ye shall not eat of every tree of the garden? And the woman said unto the serpent, We may eat of the fruit of the trees of the garden: But of the fruit of the tree which is in the midst of the garden, God hath said, Ye shall not eat of it, neither shall ye touch it, lest ye die. And the serpent said unto the woman, *Ye shall not surely die*: For God doth know that in the day ye eat thereof, then your eyes shall be opened, and ye shall be as gods, knowing good and evil. And when the woman saw that the tree was good for food, and that it was pleasant to the eyes, and a tree to be desired to make one wise, she took of the fruit thereof, and did eat, and gave also unto her husband with her; and he did eat."   Genesis 3:1-6

What territory does Satan now claim as a result of man's fall?

"*And the devil,* taking him up into a high mountain, *showed unto him all the kingdoms of the world* in a moment of time. *And the devil said unto him, All this power* will I give thee, and the glory of them: *for that is delivered unto me*; and to whomsoever I will I give it."   Luke 4:5,6

How does Satan exercise tyranny over mankind?

"*So went Satan forth* from the presence of the Lord, *and smote Job with sore boils* from the sole of his foot unto his crown."   Job 2:7

"And ought not this woman, being a daughter of Abraham, *whom Satan hath bound, lo, these eighteen years*, be loosed. . . ?"   Luke 13:16

Why is Satan increasing his efforts to ruin mankind?

"And I heard a loud voice saying in heaven, Now is come salvation, and strength, and the kingdom of our God, and the power of his Christ: *for the accuser of our brethren is cast down*, which accused them before our God day and night." "Therefore rejoice, ye heavens, and ye that dwell in them. *Woe to the inhabiters of the earth and of the sea! for the devil is come down unto you, having great wrath, because he knoweth that he hath but a short time*."   Revelation 12:10, 12

How did Jesus earn the right to finally destroy the devil?

"He that committeth sin is of the devil; for the devil sinneth from the beginning. *For this purpose the Son of God was manifested, that he might destroy the works of the devil*."   1 John 3:8

"Forasmuch then as the children are partakers of flesh and blood, he also himself likewise took part of the same; *that through death he might destroy him that had the power of death, that is, the devil*."   Hebrews 2:14

How will God ultimately destroy the devil?

"By the multitude of thy merchandise they have filled the midst of thee with violence, and thou hast sinned: therefore *I will cast thee as profane out of the mountain of God: and I will destroy thee, O covering cherub,* from the midst of the stones of fire. Thine heart was lifted up because of thy beauty, thou hast corrupted thy wisdom by reason of thy brightness: *I will cast thee to the ground, I will lay thee before kings,* that they may behold thee. Thou hast defiled thy sanctuaries by the multitude of thine iniquities, by the iniquity of thy traffic; *therefore will I bring forth a fire from the midst of thee,* it shall devour thee, and *I will bring thee to ashes upon the earth in the sight of all them that behold thee.* All they that know thee among the people shall be astonished at thee: thou shalt be a terror, and never shalt thou be any more."

Ezekiel 28:16-19

SIN ENTERS THE HUMAN FAMILY

What were God's instructions to Adam in the Garden of Eden?

"And the Lord God took the man, and put him into the garden of Eden to dress it and to keep it. *And the Lord God commanded the man, saying, Of every tree of the garden thou mayest freely eat: But of the tree of the knowledge of good and evil, thou shalt not eat of it*: for in the day that thou eatest thereof thou shalt surely die."

Genesis 2:15-17

But Adam and Eve disobeyed God.

"The serpent said unto the woman, Ye shall not surely die: For God doth know that in the day ye eat thereof, then your eyes shall be opened, and ye shall be as gods, knowing good and evil. *And when the woman saw that the tree was good for food, and that it was pleasant to the eyes, and a tree to be desired to make one wise, she took of the fruit thereof, and did eat, and gave also unto her husband with her: and he did eat."* Genesis 3:4-6

What resulted from their disobedience?

"And the Lord God said, Behold, the man is become as one of us, to know good and evil: *and now, lest he put forth his hand, and take also of the tree of life, and eat, and live for ever: Therefore the Lord God sent him forth from the garden of*

Eden, to till the ground from whence he was taken. *So he drove out the man*; and he placed at the east of the garden of Eden Cherubims, and a flaming sword which turned every way, to keep the way of the tree of life."

Genesis 3:22-24

How did sin affect the relationship between man and God?

"But *your iniquities have separated between you and your God, and your sins have hid his face from you*, that he will not hear."   Isaiah 59:2

What has been the result of Adam's sin upon all of mankind?

"Wherefore, as *by one man sin entered into the world, and death by sin; and so death passed upon all men,* for that all have sinned."

Romans 5:12

Besides Jesus, are there any other people who have never sinned?

"For all have sinned, and come short of the glory of God."   Romans 3:23

Can sinful man do anything to change his fallen condition?

"Can the Ethiopian change his skin, or the leopard his spots? *then may ye also do good, that are accustomed to do evil."*   Jeremiah 13:23

How do we obtain eternal life?

"For the wages of sin is death; but the gift of God is eternal life through Jesus Christ our Lord." Romans 6:23

Note: Eternal life is a gift, but we must accept it.

How many people is God willing to save?

"The Lord is not slack concerning His promise, as some count slackness, but is longsuffering toward us, *not willing that any should perish* but that all should come to repentance."* 2 Peter 3:9 (NKJV)

Though God is love, He is also just. God does not overlook guilt ...

"The Lord God, merciful and gracious, longsuffering, and abundant in goodness and truth, Keeping mercy for thousands, forgiving iniquity and transgression and sin, *and that will by no means clear the guilty."* Exodus 34:5-7

What plan did God devise to save sinful man?

"For God so loved the world that He gave his only begotten Son, that whosoever believeth in him should not perish, but have everlasting life."* John 3:16

Why did Jesus come to earth?

"To seek and to save that which was lost."* Luke 19:10

"He shall save his people from their sins."
                                        Matthew 1:21

What did God the Father lay on Jesus as He hung upon the cross?

"All we like sheep have gone astray, we have turned every one to his own way; and *the Lord hath laid on him the iniquity of us all."*   Isaiah 53:6

What do we have to do to receive God's grace.

"For by grace are ye saved through faith; and that not of yourselves: *it is the gift of God."*   Ephesians 2:8

What did Paul tell the jailer to do in order to be saved?

"Believe on the Lord Jesus Christ, and thou shalt be saved, and thy house."   Acts 16:31

When should we decide to receive the free gift of salvation?

"Now is the accepted time; behold, now is the day of salvation."   2 Corinthians 6:2

The Bible tells us that Jesus is knocking at the door of our hearts. What does He invite us to do?

"Behold, I stand at the door and knock: if any man hear my voice, and *open the door*, I will come in to him, and will sup with him, and he with me."
                                        Revelation 3:20

As we accept Christ into our hearts, what assurance can we have?

"He that hath the Son hath life; and he that hath not the Son of God hath not life. These things have I written unto you that believe on the name of the Son of God; *that ye may know that ye have eternal life, and that ye may believe on the name of the Son of God.*" 1 John 5:12,13

What do we become as we accept Christ as our Saviour and Lord?

"But as many as received him, *to them gave he power to become the sons of God,* even to them that believe on his name." John 1:12

JESUS, THE MAN WHO IS GOD

How long has Jesus, the Son of God, been in existence?

"But thou, Bethlehem Ephratah, though thou be little among the thousands of Judah, yet out of thee shall he come forth unto me that is to be ruler in Israel; *whose goings forth have been from of old, from everlasting.*" Micah 5:2

"And now, O Father, *glorify thou me with thine own self with the glory which I had with thee before the world was.*" John 17:5

Who is Jesus, the Word, according to the Bible?

"In the beginning was the Word, and the Word was with God, *and the Word was God.*" "And the Word was made flesh, and dwelt among us." John 1:1, 14

What does Paul say about Jesus?

"And without controversy great is the mystery of godliness: *God was manifest in the flesh,* justified in the Spirit, seen of angels, preached unto the Gentiles, believed on in the world, received up into glory." 1 Timothy 3:16

What did other witnesses say about Jesus?

a. Peter said: "Thou art the Christ, the *Son of the living God.*"   Matthew 16:16

b. The Roman Centurion said: "Truly *this was the Son of God.*"   Matthew 27:54

c. God the Father said: *"This is my beloved Son,* in whom I am well pleased."   Matthew 3:17

d. Thomas, the disciple, said: *"My Lord and my God."*   John 20:28

What part did Jesus play in the creation of this world?

"In the beginning was the Word, and the Word was with God, and the Word was God. The same was in the beginning with God. *All things were made by him; and without him was not any thing made that was made....* And the Word was made flesh, and dwelt among us."   John 1:1-3,14

"By him were all things created that are in heaven, and that are in earth, visible and invisible, whether they be thrones, or dominions, or principalities, or powers: all things were created by him, and for him."
                                                      Colossians 1:16

"God,who at sundry times and in divers manners spake in time past unto the fathers by the prophets, Hath in these last days spoken unto us by his Son, whom he hath appointed heir of all things, *by whom also he made the worlds."*   Hebrews 1:1

What did Jesus do to become our Saviour?

"Let this mind be in you, which was also in Christ Jesus: *Who, being in the form of God*, thought it not robbery to be equal with God: But made himself of no reputation, and took upon him the form of a servant, and *was made in the likeness of men*: And being found in fashion as a man, *he humbled himself, and became obedient unto death*, even the death of the cross."   Philippians 2:5-8

Why did Jesus leave heaven and come to this earth to die?

"This is a faithful saying, and worthy of all acceptation, that Christ *Jesus came into the world to save sinners;* of whom I am chief."
                                         1 Timothy 1:15

"*For the Son of man is come to seek and to save* that which was lost."   Luke 19:10

What was Mary told about Jesus?

"And the angel answered and said unto her, The Holy Ghost shall come upon thee, and the power of the Highest shall overshadow thee; therefore also *that holy thing which shall be born of thee shall be called the Son of God.*"   Luke 1:35

What did Peter say about the life of Jesus?

"How *God anointed Jesus of Nazareth with the Holy Ghost and with power*: who went about doing good, and healing all that were oppressed of the devil; *for God was with him.*"   Acts 10:38

When the disciples asked Jesus to show them the Father, what did Jesus tell them?

"Philip saith unto him, Lord, show us the Father, and it sufficeth us. Jesus saith unto him, *Have I been so long time with you, and yet hast thou not known me, Philip? he that hath seen me hath seen the Father*; and how sayest thou then, Show us the Father? Believest thou not that I am in the Father, and the Father in me?"   John 14: 8-10

What kind of life did Jesus live on earth?

"*Who did no sin, neither was guile found in his mouth:* Who, when he was reviled, reviled not again; when he suffered, he threatened not; but committed himself to him that judgeth righteously."

1 Peter 2: 22, 23

What demonstration did God make by the death of His Son?

"But God commendeth his love toward us, in that, *while we were yet sinners, Christ died for us.*"

Romans 5:8

Thought Promises:

"Neither is there salvation in any other: *for there is none other name under heaven given among men, whereby we must be saved.*"   Acts 4:12

"Behold, *what manner of love the Father hath bestowed* upon us, *that we should be called the sons of God.*"   1 John 3:1

THE WAY TO ETERNAL LIFE

How many "good" people are there on earth?

"As it is written, *there is none righteous*, no, not one."   Romans 3:10

The Apostle Paul expresses the human dilemma:

"For I know that *in me (that is, in my flesh,) dwelleth no good thing: for to will is present with me; but how to perform that which is good I find not. For the good that I would I do not: but the evil which I would not, that I do.* Now if I do that I would not, it is no more I that do it, but sin that dwelleth in me."   Romans 7:18-20

Why did Paul say that man in his natural condition cannot please God?

"Because *the carnal mind is enmity against God: for it is not subject to the law of God,* neither indeed can be. So then *they that are in the flesh cannot please God.*"   Romans 8:7, 8

What happens if we allow our sinful nature to control us?

"For *to be carnally minded is death;* but to be spiritually minded is life and peace."   Romans 8:6

Did Paul find deliverance from his sinful nature?

"O wretched man that I am! *Who shall deliver me from the body of this death? I thank God through Jesus Christ our Lord.* So then with the mind I myself serve the law of God; but with the flesh the law of sin."   Romans 7:24, 25

Faith in Christ enabled Paul to live a successful Christian life:

"I am crucified with Christ: nevertheless I live; yet not I, but Christ liveth in me: and the *life which I now live in the flesh I live by the faith of the Son of God* who loved me, and gave himself for me."
Galatians 2:20

How did Jesus describe the conversion experience?

"Verily, verily, I say unto thee, *Except a man be born again,* he cannot see the kingdom of God."
John 3:1-3

Did Nicodemus (a prominent Jew) understand what Jesus told him?

"Nicodemus saith unto him, *How can a man be born when he is old?* can he enter the second time into his mother's womb, and be born?"   John 3:4

How did Jesus explain to Nicodemus that he could be born again?

"*Jesus answered,* Verily, verily, I say unto thee, *Except a man be born of water and of the*

Spirit, he cannot enter into the kingdom of God. That which is born of the flesh is flesh; and that which is born of the Spirit is spirit. *Marvel not that I said unto thee, Ye must be born again.*"   John 3:5-7

How does God accomplish this change (conversion) in our lives?

"The wind bloweth where it listeth, and thou hearest the sound thereof, but canst not tell whence it cometh, and whither it goeth: *so is every one that is born of the Spirit.*"   John 3:8

"For *as many as are led by the Spirit of God,* they are the sons of God."   Romans 8:14

How does Paul describe the "born again" person?

"Therefore *if any man be in Christ, he is a new creature:* old things are passed away; behold, *all things are become new.*"   2 Corinthians 5:17

How does God give us the knowledge and desire to obey Him?

"For *it is God which worketh in you* both to will and to do of his good pleasure."   Philippians 2:13

"This is the covenant that I will make with them after those days, *saith the Lord, I will put my laws into their hearts, and in their minds* will I write them."   Hebrews 10:16

Will the new Christian continue to live *a life* of sin?

"What shall we say then? *Shall we continue in sin,* that grace may abound? *God forbid.* How shall we, that are dead to sin, live any longer therein? Know ye not, that so many of us as were baptized into Jesus Christ were baptized into his death? Therefore we are buried with him by baptism into death: that like *as Christ was raised up from the dead* by the glory of the Father, *even so we also should walk in newness of life.*"

Romans 6:1-4

Can we expect forgiveness if we sin after we have been born again?

"My little children, *these things write I unto you, that ye sin not. And if any man sin, we have an advocate with the Father, Jesus Christ the righteous.*"

1 John 2:1.

"*If we confess our sins, he is faithful and just to forgive us our sins,* and to cleanse us from all unrighteousness."

1 John 1:9

Thought Promise:

"I can do all things *through Christ* which strengtheneth me."

Philippians 4:13

HEAVEN WILL BE A REAL PLACE

Just before His death and resurrection, what promise did Jesus make to His followers?

"Let not your heart be troubled: ye believe in God, believe also in me. In my Father's house are many mansions: if it were not so, I would have told you. I go to prepare a place for you. *And if I go and prepare a place for you, I will come again, and receive you unto myself; that where I am, there ye may be also.*"   John 14:1-3

How does the Bible describe the "Father's house"?

"And I John saw *the holy city, new Jerusalem* ... prepared as a bride adorned for her husband."

Revelation 21:2

What description does the Bible give us of this Holy City, New Jerusalem?

a.   *"The city lieth foursquare*, and the length is as large as the breadth; and he measured the city with the reed, twelve thousand furlongs. *The length and the breadth and the height of it are equal.*"

Revelation 21:16

Note: A furlong is 1/8th of an English mile, which would mean that this city, forming a perfect square, is at least 375 miles long on each side!

126

b. "The building of the wall of it was of jasper: and *the city was pure gold, like unto clear glass.*"
Revelation 21:18

c. "The foundations of the wall of the city were *garnished with all manner of precious stones.*"
Revelation 21:19

d. "And had twelve gates . . . . and *the twelve gates were twelve pearls: every several gate was of one pearl:* and the street of the city was pure gold, as it were transparent glass."
Revelation 21:12, 21

e. *"And the city had no need of the sun, neither of the moon, to shine in it: for the glory of God did lighten it,* and the Lamb is the light thereof."
Revelation 21:23

What very special tree will be growing in the New Jerusalem, which was also found in the Garden of Eden?

a. "In the midst of the street of it, and on either side of the river, was there *the tree of life, which bare twelve manner of fruits, and yielded her fruit every month:* and the leaves of the tree were for the healing of the nations."
Revelation 22:2

b. "Therefore the Lord God sent him (Adam) forth from the garden of Eden . . . . and he placed at the east of the garden of Eden Cherubims, and a flaming sword which turned every way, to keep the way of *the tree of life.*"
Genesis 3:23, 24

God intends to make this earth the eternal home for those that are saved:

"Blessed are the meek: *for they shall inherit the earth.*"   Matthew 5:5

Note: This will occur at the end of a 1,000 year period the redeemed spend with God in heaven. A more complete explanation will be found in a succeeding study, "1,000 Years of Peace" (See pg. 179).

God will re-create the earth:

a. "Nevertheless *we, according to his promise, look for new heavens and a new earth*, wherein dwelleth righteousness."   2 Peter 3:13

b. *"And I saw a new heaven and a new earth:* for the first heaven and the first earth were passed away; and there was no more sea."   Revelation 21:1

God will transport His capital city, the New Jerusalem, to earth!

"*And I John saw the holy city, new Jerusalem, coming down from God out of heaven,* prepared as a bride adorned for her husband. And I heard a great voice out of heaven saying, Behold, the tabernacle of God is with men, and he will dwell with them, and they shall be his people, and God himself shall be with them, and be their God.   Revelation 21:2, 3

The earth, made new, will be perfect!

a. "*Then the eyes of the blind shall be opened, and the ears of the deaf shall be unstopped. Then shall the lame man leap as a hart, and the tongue of the dumb sing:*

for in the wilderness shall waters break out, and streams in the desert." Isaiah 35:5, 6

b. *"The wolf and the lamb shall feed together, and the lion shall eat straw like the bullock . . .* They shall not hurt nor destroy in all my holy mountain, saith the Lord." Isaiah 65:25

c. *"They shall hunger no more, neither thirst any more;* neither shall the sun light on them, nor any heat." Revelation 7:16

d. *"And God shall wipe away all tears from their eyes;* and there shall be no more death, neither sorrow, nor crying, neither shall there be any more pain." Revelation 21:4

God's redeemed people will be satisfied!

"And they shall build houses, and inhabit them, and they shall plant vineyards, and eat the fruit of them. They shall not build, and another inhabit; they shall not plant, and another eat: for as the days of a tree are the days of my people, and *mine elect shall long enjoy the work of their hands."*

Isaiah 65:21, 22

They will worship and praise God:

"And it shall come to pass, that from one new moon to another, and from one sabbath to another, *shall all flesh come to worship before Me, saith the Lord."* Isaiah 66:23

According to Jesus, in heaven we will become acquainted with other Bible characters:

"And I say unto you, That *many shall come from the east and west, and shall sit down with Abraham, and Isaac, and Jacob, in the kingdom of heaven.*"   Matthew 8:11

According to the Apostle Paul, friends will meet and recognize each other in heaven:

"For now we see through a glass, darkly; *but then face to face*: now I know in part; but *then shall I know even as also I am known.*"

1 Corinthians 13:12

Thought promise:

"Eye hath not seen, nor ear heard, neither have entered into the heart of man, the things which God hath prepared for them that love him."   1 Corinthians 2:9

JESUS WILL COME AGAIN!

Under oath, what declaration did Jesus make to the High Priest at His trial?

"Jesus saith unto him, Thou hast said: nevertheless I say unto you, *Hereafter shall ye see the Son of man sitting on the right hand of power, and coming in the clouds of heaven*." Matthew 26:64

Why will Jesus return?

"I go to prepare a place for you. And if I go and prepare a place for you, *I will come again, and receive you unto myself; that where I am, there ye may be also*." John 14:1-3

Is there another reason for His second coming?

a. "For the Son of man shall come in the glory of his Father with his angels, *and then he shall reward every man according to his works*."
Matthew 16:27

b. "And, behold, *I come quickly; and my reward is with me, to give every man according as his work shall be*." Revelation 22:12

His Coming Will Be Literal!

According to heavenly angels, how will Christ return to this earth?

"And when he had spoken these things, while they beheld, *he was taken up; and a cloud received him out of their sight*.   And while they (the disciples) looked stedfastly toward heaven as he went up, behold, two men stood by them in white apparel. Which also said, Ye men of Galilee, why stand ye gazing up into heaven? *this same Jesus, which is taken up from you into heaven, shall so come in like manner as ye have seen him go into heaven*." Acts 1:9-11

His Coming Will Be Visible!

Everyone living at the time of Jesus' return will see Him coming:

a. "*Behold, he cometh with clouds; and every eye shall see him*, and they also which pierced him: and all kindreds of the earth shall wail because of him. Even so, Amen."   Revelation 1:7

b. "And the kings of the earth, and the great men, and the rich men, and the chief captains, and the mighty men, and every bondman, and every free man, hid themselves in the dens and in the rocks of the mountains; *And said to the mountains and rocks, Fall on us, and hide us from the face of him that sitteth on the throne, and from the wrath of the Lamb*: For the great day of his wrath is come; and who shall be able to stand?"   Revelation 6:15-17

His Coming Will Be Audible!

What triumphal sounds shake the earth as Jesus comes?

"For the Lord himself shall descend from heaven with *a shout*, with *the voice of the archangel*, and with *the trump of God*: and the dead in Christ shall rise first."   1 Thessalonians 4:16

How does Peter describe the deafening sound of that momentous day when Jesus returns?

"But *the day of the Lord will come* as a thief in the night; *in the which the heavens shall pass away with a great noise*, and the elements shall melt with fervent heat, the earth also and the works that are therein shall be burned up."   2 Peter 3:10

Immediate, Dramatic Changes Will Occur At His Coming!

What thrilling change takes place as Christ returns?

"Behold, I show you a mystery: We shall not all sleep, but *we shall all be changed, In a moment, in the twinkling of an eye*, at the last trump: for the trumpet shall sound, and *the dead shall be raised incorruptible, and we shall be changed*."

1 Corinthians 15:51, 52

What instruction will Jesus give to the angels when He appears?

"And then shall appear the sign of the Son of man in heaven: and then shall all the tribes of the earth mourn, and they shall see the Son of man coming in the clouds of heaven with power and great glory. *And he shall send his angels with a great sound of a trumpet, and they shall gather together his elect from the four winds, from one end of heaven to the other.*"   Matthew 24:30, 31

What happens to the living, righteous saints when Christ appears?

"*Then we which are alive and remain shall be caught up together with them in the clouds,* to meet the Lord in the air: and so shall we ever be with the Lord."   1 Thessalonians 4:17

There will be a mighty earthquake:

"*There was a great earthquake* . . . And the heaven departed as a scroll when it is rolled together; and *every mountain and island were moved out of their places.*"   Revelation 6:12, 14

His Coming Will Be Glorious!

To what can we compare the glory and brightness of Christ's coming?

"For *as the lightning* cometh out of the east, and shineth even unto the west; *so shall also the coming of the Son of man be.*"   Matthew 24:27

Whose glory will add to the splendor of Christ at His Second Coming?

"For whosoever shall be ashamed of me and of my words, of him shall the Son of man be ashamed, *when he shall come in his own glory, and in his Father's and of the holy angels.*"   Luke 9:26

A Warning of Counterfeit Christs!

What specific warning did Jesus give so His followers would not be deceived?

a. *"Wherefore if they shall say unto you, Behold, he is in the desert; go not forth: behold, he is in the secret chambers; believe it not.* For as the lightning cometh out of the east, and shineth even unto the west; so shall also the coming of the Son of man be."

Matthew 24:26, 27

b. "For *there shall arise false Christs, and false prophets*, and shall show great signs and wonders; *insomuch that, if it were possible, they shall deceive the very elect.*"

Matthew 24:24

His Coming Will Be Unexpected!

Who only knows the day and hour of the Second Coming of Jesus?

"*But of that day and hour knoweth no man*, no, not the angels of heaven, *but my Father only.*"

Matthew 24:36

Why should we be always ready for Jesus' return?

a. "Therefore be ye also ready: *for in such an hour as ye think not the Son of man cometh.*"

Matthew 24:44

b. "*And take heed to yourselves,* lest at any time your hearts be overcharged with surfeiting, and drunkenness, and cares of this life, and so that day come upon you unawares. *For as a snare shall it come on all them that dwell on the face of the whole earth. Watch ye therefore, and pray always.*"

Luke 21:34-36

Thought Promises:

"Beloved, now are we the sons of God, and *it doth not yet appear what we shall be: but we know that, when he shall appear, we shall be like him; for we shall see him as he is.* And every man that hath this hope in him purifieth himself, even as he is pure."

1 John 3:2, 3

"And it shall be said in that day, *Lo, this is our God*; we have waited for him, and *he will save us: this is the Lord*; we have waited for him, *we will be glad and rejoice in his salvation.*"

Isaiah 25:9

TIME IS RUNNING OUT

What question did the disciples ask Jesus concerning the end of the world?

"And as he sat upon the mount of Olives, *the disciples came unto him privately, saying, Tell us, when shall these things be? and what shall be the sign of thy coming, and of the end of the world?*"

Matthew 24:3

Here are some of the signs Jesus said would occur at the end of the world:

War And Bloodshed

"And ye shall hear of *wars and rumors of wars*: see that ye be not troubled: for all these things must come to pass, but the end is not yet. *For nation shall rise against nation, and kingdom against kingdom:*

Natural Disasters And Calamities

"and *there shall be famines, and pestilences, and earthquakes,* in divers places. All these are the beginning of sorrows.

Religious Persecution

"Then shall *they deliver you up to be afflicted, and shall kill you:* and ye shall be hated of all nations for my name's sake. *And then shall many be offended, and shall betray one another, and shall hate one another.*

False Prophets And Teachers, Immorality And Divorce

"And many false prophets shall rise, and shall deceive many. *And because iniquity shall abound, the love of many shall wax cold."*

Matthew 24: 6-12

Additional signs of the "end times":

Economic Woes

Go to now, *ye rich men, weep and howl for your miseries that shall come upon you.* Your riches are corrupted, and your garments are moth-eaten. Your gold and silver is cankered . . . *ye have heaped treasure together for the last days."*   James 5:1-3

A Selfish And Proud Generation At The End. . .

"This know also, that in the last days perilous times shall come. For men shall be lovers of their own selves, covetous, boasters, proud, blasphemers, disobedient to parents, unthankful, unholy. Without natural affection, trucebreakers, false accusers, incontinent, fierce, despisers of those that are good, Traitors, heady, highminded, lovers of pleasures more than lovers of God; Having a form of godliness, but denying the power thereof: from such turn away."   2 Timothy 3:1-5

Two prophetic writings are to be given special attention at the time of the end:

a. *"But you, O Daniel, shut up the words and seal the Book until the time of the end.* (Then) many shall run to and fro and search anxiously (through the Book), *and knowledge* (of God's purposes as revealed by His prophets) *shall be increased and become great."*

(Amplified Bible) Daniel 12:4

b. *"The Revelation of Jesus Christ,* which God gave unto him, *to show unto his servants things which must shortly come to pass....* Blessed is he that readeth, and they that hear the words of this prophecy, and keep those things which are written therein . . ."

Revelation 1:1, 3

Note: Two prophetic writings are widely recognized as apocalyptic (that is having to do with the end of time); the book of Daniel in the Old Testament and the book of Revelation in the New Testament.

What did Jesus say about Daniel's prophecy and events at the end of time?

"When ye (Christ's followers at the end) *therefore shall see the abomination of desolation, spoken of by Daniel the prophet,* stand in the holy place, (whoso readeth, let him understand:) Then let them which be in Judea flee into the mountains . . . . *For then shall be great tribulation* . . . . Then if any man shall say unto you, Lo, here is Christ, or there; believe it not. For there shall arise false Christs, and false prophets, and shall show great signs and wonders; insomuch that, if it were possible, they shall deceive the very elect."   Matthew 24:15, 16, 21, 23, 24

What special message found in the book of Revelation will be preached to the whole world just before Christ returns?

"And I saw another angel fly in the midst of heaven, *having the everlasting gospel to preach unto them that dwell on the earth, and to every nation, and kindred, and tongue, and people, Saying with a loud voice, Fear God, and give glory to him; for the hour of his judgment is come;* and worship him that made heaven, and earth, and the sea, and the fountains of waters."   Revelation 14:6, 7

What events will mark the climax of earth's final crisis?

"And *there shall be signs in the sun, and in the moon, and in the stars; and upon the earth distress of nations, with perplexity*; the sea and the waves roaring; Men's hearts failing them for fear, and for looking after those things which are coming on the earth: *for the powers of heaven shall be shaken. And then shall they see the Son of man coming in a cloud with power and great glory."*   Luke 21:25-27

What should God's redeemed do when all these signs come to pass?

"And when these things begin to come to pass, then look up, and lift up your heads; for your redemption draweth nigh."   Luke 21:28

What final admonition did Jesus offer His followers?

"*And take heed to yourselves,* lest at any time your hearts be overcharged with surfeiting, and drunkenness, and cares of this life, and so that day come upon you unawares . . . . *Watch ye therefore, and pray always, that ye may be accounted worthy to escape all these things that shall come to pass,* and to stand before the Son of man."

Luke 21:34, 36

WHAT ABOUT GOD'S LAW?

What was Christ's attitude toward God's law?

"*I delight to do thy will*, O my God: yea, *thy law is within my heart.*" Psalm 40:8

How did Jesus address God's law in His most famous sermon?

"*Think not that I am come to destroy the law*, or the prophets: *I am not come to destroy, but to fulfil.* For verily I say unto you, *Till heaven and earth pass, one jot or one tittle shall in no wise pass from the law*, till all be fulfilled." Matthew 5:17,18

How did God make His law known?

"And he gave unto Moses, when he had made an end of communing with him upon mount Sinai, *two tables of testimony, tables of stone, written with the finger of God.*" Exodus 31:18

Note these facts about God's law:

a. No human element was involved in the formulating of the Ten Commandments as found in Exodus 20:1-17. Everything else in the Bible was written by the prophets. Not so with the Ten Commandments! If some parts of the Word of God were purer than others, this would be the ultimate!

142

Government cannot exist without law and order. Society cannot function without rules. Men cannot do business without certain guidelines. Children cannot play games without rules. Even Nature has her laws! Should we be surprised then that God governs His Universe by law?

b. The Ten Commandment law, *written on stone by God's own finger, was placed INSIDE* the ark.

"At that time the Lord said unto me, Hew thee two tables of stone like unto the first . . . . And I will write on the tables the words, that were in the first tables which thou brakest, *and thou shalt put them in the ark* . . . . And he wrote on the tables . . . the ten commandments . . . and the Lord gave them unto me. *And I . . . came down from the mount, and put the tables in the ark which I had made."*

Deuteronomy 10:1 5

c. A second "law" was *written by Moses in a book (instead of on stone), and placed IN THE SIDE of the ark.*

"And it came to pass, when Moses had made an end of writing the words of this law in a book, until they were finished, That Moses commanded the Levites, which bare the ark of the covenant of the Lord, saying, *Take this book of the law, and put it in the side of the ark of the covenant of the Lord your God,* that it may be there for a witness against thee."

Deuteronomy 31:24-26

A Comparison of
God's Law and Moses' Law

God's Law	Moses' Law
Called "The Law of the Lord" Isaiah 5:24	Called "the law of Moses" Luke 2:22 1 Corinthians 9:9
Written by God on stone Exodus 31:18; 32:16	Written by Moses in a book 2 Chronicles 35:12 Deuteronomy 31:24
Placed inside the ark Deuteronomy 10:2, 5	Placed in the side of the ark Deuteronomy 31:26
Points out sin Romans 7:7; 3:20	Added because of sin Galatians 3:19
Not grievous 1 John 5:3	Contrary to us Colossians 2:14
Called "The Royal Law" James 2:8	Called "Law contained In ordinances" Ephesians 2:15
Judges all men James 2:10-12	Judges no man Colossians 2:14-16
Spiritual Romans 7:14	Carnal Hebrews 7:16
Perfect Psalms 19:7	Made nothing perfect Hebrews 7:19

What is the purpose of the law of God?

"What shall we say then? Is the law sin? God forbid. Nay, *I had not known sin, but by the law:* for I had not known lust, except the law had said, Thou shalt not covet."   Romans 7:7

What is the purpose of the law of Moses?

"Wherefore then serveth the law? *It was added because of transgressions.*"   Galatians 3:19

Note: Unfortunately, Paul does not differentiate between the two laws, but refers only to the "law". As a result many have concluded that God's law (Ten Commandments), has been done away with. However, as we read the context, we can readily discern which law Paul was referring to since he states that it was "written in the book of the law" and not on stone (See Galatians 3:10).

Those who love God and their fellow man, fulfill (keep) the Law of God!

Jesus said:

"Thou shalt love the Lord thy God with all thy heart, and with all thy soul, and with all thy mind. *This is the first and great commandment. And the second is like unto it,* Thou shalt love thy neighbor as thyself. *On these two commandments hang all the law* and the prophets.

                    Matthew 22:37-40

Note: Some theorize that the Ten Commandments are the Father's, while Christ's commandments are just two, totally unrelated to the Ten Commandments of the Old Testament. A careful study of the Ten Commandments however, reveals that the first four deal with our love toward God, while the last six deal with our relationship to our neighbor. This is why Jesus said, "On these two commandments hang all the law". The Father's commandments and Christ's commandments are one and the same!

"*If ye keep my commandments, ye shall abide in my love;* even as I have kept my Father's commandments, and abide in his love."   John 15:10

"*Whosoever therefore shall break one of these least commandments, and shall teach men so, he shall be called the least in the kingdom of heaven: but whosoever shall do and teach them, the same shall be called great in the kingdom of heaven.*"   Matthew 5:19

"If thou wilt enter into life, *keep the commandments.*"   Matthew 19:17

Paul wrote:

"Owe no man any thing, but to love one another: *for he that loveth another hath fulfilled the law.* For this, Thou shalt not commit adultery, Thou shalt not kill, Thou shalt not steal, Thou shalt not bear false witness, Thou shalt not covet; and if there by any other commandment, it is briefly comprehended in this saying, namely, Thou shalt love thy neighbor as thyself. Love worketh no ill to his neighbor: *therefore love is the fulfilling of the law.*"   Romans 13:8-10

The Bible Conclusion:

Old Testament

"Let us hear the conclusion of the whole matter: *Fear God and keep his commandments: for this is the whole duty of man.*"   Ecclesiastes 12:13

New Testament

"*For whosoever shall keep the whole law, and yet offend in one point, he is guilty of all.* For he that said, Do not commit adultery, said also, Do not kill. Now if thou commit no adultery, yet if thou kill, thou art become a transgressor of the law. So speak ye, and so do, as they that shall be judged by the law of liberty."   James 2:10-12

LAW AND GRACE

What is the Bible definition of sin?

"Whosoever committeth sin transgresseth also the law: *for sin is the transgression of the law.*"

1 John 3:4

How many have sinned?

"For all have sinned, and come short of the glory of God."
Romans 3:23

What have all sinners earned?

"For the wages of sin is death. . . "
Romans 6:23

How then does God save sinners?

a. "For the wages of sin is death; but *the gift of God is eternal life* through Jesus Christ our Lord."
Romans 6:23

b. *"For by grace are ye saved through faith; and that not of yourselves: it is the gift of God:* Not of works, lest any man should boast."
Ephesians 2:8, 9

According to Paul, what does our faith in Christ do to the law of God?

"Do we then make void the law through faith? God forbid: yea, we establish the law."
Romans 3:31

If we keep the law, does this save us?

"Therefore *by the deeds of the law there shall no flesh be justified* in his sight. . .   Romans 3:20

Then what purpose does the law serve?

"Therefore by the deeds of the law there shall no flesh be justified in his sight: *for by the law is the knowledge of sin.*"   Romans 3:20

If the law only points out sin, how is it then, that we can be cleansed and saved from our sins?

"*But if we walk in the light, as he is in the light,* we have fellowship one with another, and *the blood of Jesus Christ his Son cleanseth us from all sin.*"   1 John 1:7

Note: The law can only point out sin in our lives. It cannot forgive us for that sin. Forgiveness can only come through the sacrifice of Jesus. James 1:23-25 tells us that while a mirror may show us what we look like, the mirror will not remove any dirt that may be on our face! We need to wash our face with soap and water in order to be clean. When it comes to sin, God's law is the mirror that reveals it, and Jesus' cleansing blood removes it!

Does grace give us license to break God's Law?

"*What shall we say then?   Shall we continue in sin, that grace may abound?   God forbid.* How shall we, that are dead to sin, live any longer therein?" "For sin shall not have dominion over you: for ye are not under the law, but under grace. *What*

*then? shall we sin, because we are not under
the law, but under grace?   God forbid."*
Romans 6:1,2,14,15

*Note: Sin is defined as the transgression of God's law.
Jesus came to save us from our sins, not in them. Grace
is not a license to sin; it is the power that God gives that
we may be able to stop sinning.*

What has our Heavenly Father promised regarding His law?

"For this is the covenant that I will make with the
house of Israel after those days, saith the Lord; *I will
put my laws into their mind, and write them in
their hearts:* and I will be to them a God, and they shall
be to me a people."
Hebrews 8:10

What special blessing is pronounced in the last chapter of the Bible?

*"Blessed   are   they   that   do   His
commandments, that they may have right to
the Tree of Life, and may enter in through the
gates into the city."*
Revelation 22:14

Thought promise:

"Not every one that saith unto me, Lord, Lord,
*shall enter into the kingdom of heaven; but he
that doeth the will of my Father* which is in
heaven."
Matthew 7:21

A Day To Remember

God created the heavens and the earth in six days. What did He do on the *seventh day* to make it His special day?

a. "And *on the seventh day God ended his work* which he had made;

b. *he rested on the seventh day* from all his work which he had made.

c. *God blessed the seventh day, and sanctified it.*"

Genesis 2:2, 3

Which day is the seventh day?

The Dictionary's answer:

"Seventh day, Saturday, the seventh day of the week" (Webster's New Twentieth Century Dictionary, Unabridged Second Edition, 1973).

Throughout the Bible, what unique expression or name is given to the seventh day?

"In six days the Lord made heaven and earth, the sea, and all that in them is, and rested the seventh day: wherefore the Lord blessed *the Sabbath day,* and hallowed it."

Exodus 20:11

According to Scripture, to whom does this day belong?

"Remember the Sabbath day to keep it holy. Six days shalt thou labor, and do all thy work: but *the seventh day is the Sabbath of the Lord thy God:* in it thou shalt not do any work." Exodus 20:8-10

Note: In a previous lesson, the importance of God's Ten Commandments has been noted. God wrote them with His own finger.   A simple reading of the Ten Commandments will reveal how many words God devoted to the Sabbath Commandment (4th Commandment) as compared with the other nine.

Think It Through

COMPARE

	THE LAW OF GOD	Commandment	Words Used
I	"Thou shalt have no other gods before Me."	1	8
II	"Thou shalt not make unto thee any graven image, or any likeness of anything that is in heaven above, or that is in the earth beneath, or that is in the water under the earth. Thou shalt not bow down thyself to them, nor serve them, for I the Lord thy God am a jealous God, visiting the iniquity of the fathers upon the children unto the third and fourth generation of them that hate Me; and showing mercy unto thousands of them that love Me, and keep My commandments."	2	91
III	"Thou shalt not take the name of the Lord thy God in vain; for the Lord will not hold him guiltless that taketh His name in vain."	3	27
IV	"Remember the Sabbath day, to keep it holy. Six days shalt thou labor, and do all thy work; but the seventh day is the Sabbath of the Lord thy God. In it thou shalt not do any work, thou, nor thy son, nor thy daughter, thy manservant, nor thy maidservant, nor thy cattle, nor thy stranger that is within thy gates. For in six days the Lord made heaven and earth, the sea, and all that in them is, and rested the seventh day. Wherefore the Lord blessed the Sabbath day, and hallowed it."	4	(94)
V	"Honor thy father and thy mother, that thy days may be long upon the land which the Lord thy God giveth thee."	5	22
VI	"Thou shalt not kill."	6	4
VII	"Thou shalt not commit adultery."	7	5
VIII	"Thou shalt not steal."	8	4
IX	"Thou shalt not bear false witness against thy neighbor."	9	9
X	"Thou shalt not covet thy neighbor's house; thou shalt not covet thy neighbor's wife, nor his manservant, nor his maidservant, nor his ox, nor his ass, nor anything that is thy neighbor's." -Exodus 20:3-17	10	33

What three specific commands are encompassed in the fourth commandment?

1. *"Remember the Sabbath day, to keep it holy."* Exodus 20:8

2. *"Six days shalt thou labor. . ."* Exodus 20:9

3. *"In it* (the Sabbath) *thou shalt do no labor."* Exodus 20:10

Think It Through:

Jesus' Words:
a. *"I have kept my Father's Commandments,* and abide in his love." John 15:10

Jesus' Example:
b. "And he came to Nazareth, where he had been brought up: and, *as his custom was, he went into the synagogue on the Sabbath day,* and stood up for to read." Luke 4:16

c. *"Jesus Christ the same yesterday, and today, and for ever."* Hebrews 13:8

According to the New Testament, who created all things?

a. "God, who at sundry times and in divers manners spake in time past unto the fathers by the prophets, Hath in these last days *spoken unto us by his Son,* whom he hath appointed heir of all things, *by whom also he made the worlds."* Hebrews 1:1, 2

b. "In the beginning was the Word, and the Word was with God, and the Word was God . . . . *All things were made by him* . . . . He was in the world, and the world was made by him, and the world knew him not. He came unto his own, and his own received him not . . . . *And the Word was made flesh and dwelt among us."*   John 1:1, 3, 10, 11, 14

Note: Jesus created our world. The Creator Himself came to die for us. One who is equal with God, for He is God. By remembering to keep the Sabbath holy, we acknowledge our faith in Jesus, not only as our Saviour, but also as Creator.

Which day of the week did the Apostle Paul keep holy?

"And Paul, as his manner was, went in unto them, and three Sabbath days reasoned with them out of the scriptures."   Acts 17:2

Did Paul teach both Jews and Gentiles on the Sabbath?

"And he (Paul) reasoned in the synagogue every Sabbath, and persuaded the Jews and the Greeks . . . . And he continued there a year and six months, teaching the word of God among them."
                   Acts 18:4, 11

According to the book of Acts, when did the Gentiles request that the truth of Christ be presented to them?

"And when the Jews were gone out of the synagogue, the Gentiles besought that these words might be preached to them the next Sabbath . . . . *And the next Sabbath day came almost the whole city together to hear the word of God."*
                   Acts 13:42, 44

So many centuries have passed, can Christians today be certain just which day is the seventh day of the week?

The Bible Answer:

a. "This man went unto Pilate, and begged the body of Jesus. And he took it down, and wrapped it in linen, and laid it in a sepulchre that was hewn in stone, wherein never man before was laid. *And that day was the preparation, and the Sabbath drew on.*" Luke 23:52-54

Note: Christ died on "Good Friday." Friday, the sixth day of the week was called the preparation day by the Jews. They were to prepare for the Sabbath which would begin at sundown on Friday. God's creation days began with the evening or dark part first; the daylight portion followed. (Genesis 1:5-31). Hence God's instruction to observe Sabbath from "even (evening) unto even." (See Leviticus 23:32; also Mark 1:21, 32).

b. "And the women also, which came with him from Galilee, followed after, and beheld the sepulcher, and how his body was laid. *And they returned, and prepared spices and ointments; and rested the Sabbath day according to the commandment.*" Luke 23:55-56

Note: The closest followers of Christ observed the Sabbath at His death and afterward. Jesus Himself rested in the tomb over the Sabbath hours, keeping God's Commandments even in His death!

c. "And they returned, . . . *and rested the sabbath day according to the commandment.* Now upon *the first day of the week*, very early in the morning, they came unto the sepulcher. . . . and found not the body of Jesus." Luke 23: 56; 24:1, 3

Note: This scripture passage is very helpful in establishing the fact that the seventh day of the week, the day we call "Saturday" — is the seventh day of the week mentioned in the Bible, the day called "The Sabbath" (see Mark 16:1, 2).

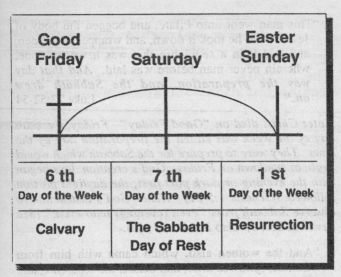

Good Friday	Saturday	Easter Sunday
6 th Day of the Week	**7 th** Day of the Week	**1 st** Day of the Week
Calvary	The Sabbath Day of Rest	Resurrection

Sabbath Facts:

The Sabbath was given to be a blessing to mankind:

"And he said unto them, *The Sabbath was made for man, and not man for the Sabbath.*"

Mark 2:27

The Sabbath is the Lord's day:

"Therefore *the Son of man is Lord also of the Sabbath.*"

Mark 2:28

The Sabbath is not for work or business:

"In those days saw I in Judah *some treading wine presses on the Sabbath* . . . and I testified against them . . . . which brought fish, and all manner of ware, *and sold on the Sabbath* unto the children of Judah, and in Jerusalem. Then I . . . said unto them, *What evil thing is this that ye do, and profane the Sabbath day?*"   Nehemiah 13:15-17

The Sabbath is not for secular pleasure seeking but a day for spiritual pursuits:

"*If thou turn away thy foot from the Sabbath, from doing thy pleasure on my holy day; and call the Sabbath a delight, the holy of the Lord, honorable; and shalt honor him, not doing thine own ways, nor finding thine own pleasure, nor speaking thine own words: Then shalt thou delight thyself in the Lord;* and I will cause thee to ride upon the high places of the earth, and feed thee with the heritage of Jacob thy father: for the mouth of the Lord hath spoken it."   Isaiah 58:13, 14

When Jesus creates the new earth, what will we do on the Sabbath?

"*For as the new heavens and the new earth, which I will make, shall remain before me, saith the Lord . . . . it shall come to pass, that from . . . one Sabbath to another, shall all flesh come to worship before me, saith the Lord.*"

Isaiah 66:22, 23

What did Jesus say is lawful to do on the Sabbath?

"He went into their synagogue: And, behold, there was a man which had his hand withered. And they asked him, saying, Is it lawful to heal on the Sabbath days? that they might accuse him. And he said unto them, What man shall there be among you, that shall have one sheep, and if it fall into a pit on the Sabbath day, will he not lay hold on it, and lift it out? How much then is a man better than a sheep? *Wherefore it is lawful to do well on the Sabbath days.*"   Matthew 12:9-13

Thought Promises:

"But whoso keepeth his word, in him verily is the love of God perfected: hereby know we that we are in him. *He that saith he abideth in him ought himself also so to walk, even as he walked."*   1 John 2:5, 6

"For this is the love of God, that we keep his commandments: and his commandments are not grievous."   1 John 5:3

HOW DID SUNDAY BECOME THE POPULAR DAY?

What vow did God make?

"My covenant will I not break, nor alter the thing that is gone out of my lips."

Psalm 89:34

What is God's unbreakable covenant?

"And he declared unto you his covenant, which he commanded you to perform, even ten commandments: and he wrote them upon two tables of stone." Deuteronomy 4:13

Note: God vowed that He would never alter or change His Covenant Law. If any change has been attempted, it certainly was not done by Jesus, for He Himself said, "Think not that I am come to destroy the law, or the prophets: I am not come to destroy, but to fulfill. For verily I say unto you, Till heaven and earth pass, one jot or one tittle shall in no wise pass from the law, till all be fulfilled. Whosoever therefore shall break one of these least commandments, and shall teach men so, he shall be called the least in the kingdom of heaven: but whosoever shall do and teach them, the same shall be called great in the kingdom of heaven." Matthew 5:17-19.

Eight New Testament Texts

Note: In the Bible, Sunday is always referred to as the first day of the week, and there are only eight Scripture references in the New Testament which mention the first day of the week. If there is a command to keep Sunday holy it should be found in one of these Bible passages.

Below are five New Testament *first day* texts. Do any of these texts suggest that Sunday, the first day of the week, is to be considered holy?

1. "In the end of the Sabbath, as it began to dawn toward *the first day of the week,* came Mary Magdalene and the other Mary to see the sepulcher."
Matthew 28:1

2. "And when the Sabbath was past, Mary Magdalene, and Mary the mother of James, and Salome, had bought sweet spices, that they might come and anoint him. And very early in the morning *the first day of the week,* they came unto the sepulcher at the rising of the sun."
Mark 16:1, 2

3. "Now when Jesus was risen early *the first day of the week,* he appeared first to Mary Magdalene, out of whom he had cast seven devils."
Mark 16:9

4. "Now upon *the first day of the week,* very early in the morning, they came unto the sepulcher, bringing the spices which they had prepared, and certain others with them."
Luke 24:1

5. *"The first day of the week* cometh Mary Magdalene early, when it was yet dark, unto the sepulcher, and seeth the stone taken away from the sepulcher."
John 20:1

The sixth *first day* text involves a gathering of the disciples on the evening of the resurrection day. According to the passage, why were they assembled?

6. "Then the same day at evening, being *the first day of the week,* when the doors were shut where *the disciples were assembled for fear of the Jews,* came Jesus and stood in the midst, and saith unto them, Peace be unto you."   John 20:19

Note: Some claim the disciples had gathered to keep holy the first day of the week in honor of the resurrection. However, Mark explains that the disciples did not even believe Jesus had been raised from the dead until He appeared in their midst that evening! "Afterward he appeared unto the eleven . . . and upbraided them with their unbelief and hardness of heart, because they believed not them which had seen him after he was risen." Mark 16:14.

The seventh *first day* text involves contributions requested by Paul for the poor:

7. "Now concerning the collection for the saints . . . . Upon *the first day of the week let every one of you lay by him in store,* as God hath prospered him, *that there be no gatherings when I come."*   1 Corinthians 16:1, 2

Note: Paul was not suggesting changing the Sabbath in order to receive a public collection at a Sunday service. Rather, Paul's desire was that collections be done during the week so that he could devote more time to teaching and preaching on Sabbath!

The eighth, and final *first day* text, deals with a farewell meeting Paul held on the first day of the week:

8. "And upon *the first day of the week, when the disciples came together to break bread, Paul preached unto them, ready to depart on the morrow; and continued his speech until midnight.* And there were many lights in the upper chamber, where they were gathered together."   Acts 20:7, 8

Note: The fact that the disciples broke bread at this meeting does not indicate that the day was holy, since the early believers broke bread every day of the week: "And they, continuing daily . . . breaking bread from house to house, did eat their meat with gladness." Acts 2:46. Notice also that the meeting took place at night since verse 8 says, "There were many lights in the upper chamber." In the previous lesson, it was noted that a day, according to the Bible, is measured from sundown to sundown. (See note on page 155). The dark part of the day, or evening, comes first in the Bible, then comes the light part, (Genesis 1:5, 8, 13). Paul called this meeting for the dark part of Sunday, which is what we now call Saturday night. The Good News Bible translates this text as follows: "On Saturday evening we gathered together for the fellowship meal. Paul spoke to the people and kept speaking until midnight, Saturday night, since he planned to leave the next day." The book of Acts records eighty-four Sabbath meetings, but only one Saturday night meeting. Should this be construed as a command to change the day of worship?

But most Christians observe Sunday rather than Sabbath; when did the change take place?

Note: Early in the fourth century A.D., the Emperor Constantine issued a decree making Sunday a public festival throughout the Roman Empire. The day of the sun (SUNday) was reverenced by his pagan subjects and was honored by some Christians. "It was the emperor's policy to unite the conflicting interests of heathenism and Christianity. He was urged to do this by the bishops of the church, who, inspired by ambition and thirst for power, perceived that if the same day was observed by both Christians and heathen, it would promote the nominal acceptance of Christianity by pagans and thus advance the power and glory of the church." E. G. White, The Great Controversy, page 53.

Afterward, in the year 364 A.D., at the Council of Laodicea, the Catholic Church approved the change of the day of worship and commanded everyone to keep Sunday as the holy day instead of Saturday.

Question: What challenge do Catholics give to Protestants concerning Sunday?

Answer: "The Church changed the observance of the Sabbath to Sunday by rite of the divine, infallible authority given to her by her founder, Jesus Christ. The Protestant, claiming the Bible to be the only guide of faith, has no warrant for observing Sunday." *The Catholic Universe Bulletin*, August 14, 1942.

Question: Have you any other way of proving that the Church has power to institute festivals of precept?

Answer: "Had she not such power, she could not have done that in which all modern religionists agree with her—she could not have substituted the observance of Sunday, the first day of the week, for the observance of Saturday, the seventh day, a change for which there is no Scriptural authority." Rev. Stephan Keenan, *A Doctrinal Catechism*, page 174.

"CATHOLICISM SPEAKS"

"Sunday is a Catholic institution, and its claims to observance can be defended only on Catholic principles . . . From beginning to end of scripture there is not a single passage that warrants the transfer of weekly public worship from the last day of the week to the first."   *- Catholic Press, Sydney, Australia, August, 1900*

"Protestantism, in discarding the authority of the (Roman Catholic) Church, has no good reasons for its Sunday theory, and ought logically to keep Saturday as the Sabbath."

- John Gilmary Shea, in the "American Catholic Quarterly Review," January 1883

"It is well to remind the Presbyterians, Baptists, Methodists, and all other Christians, that the Bible does not support them anywhere in their observance of Sunday. Sunday is an institution of the Roman Catholic Church, and those who observe the day observe a commandment of the Catholic Church."

- Priest Brady, in an address, reported in the Elizabeth, N.J. "News" of March 18, 1903

"Ques. - Have you any other way of proving that the (Catholic) Church has power to institute festivals of precept (to command holy days)?"

"Ans. - Had she not such power, she could not have done that in which all modern religionists agree with her: she could not have substituted the observance of Sunday the first day of the week, for the observance of Saturday the seventh day, a change for which there is no Scriptural authority."

- Stephan Keenan, "A Doctrinal Catechism," p. 176

"Reason and common sense demand the acceptance of one or the other of these alternatives: either Protestantism and the keeping holy of Saturday, or Catholicity and the keeping holy of Sunday. Compromise is impossible."

- "The Catholic Mirror," December 23, 1893

"God simply gave His (Catholic) Church the power to set aside whatever day or days, she would deem suitable as Holy Days. The Church chose Sunday, the first day of the week, and in the course of time added other days, as holy days."   *-Vincent J. Kelly, "Forbidden Sunday and Feast-Day Occupations," p. 2*

"Protestants . . accept Sunday rather than Saturday as the day for public worship after the Catholic Church made the change . . . But the Protestant mind does not seem to realize that . . . in observing the Sunday, they are accepting the authority of the spokesman for the church, the Pope."

- "Our Sunday Visitor," February 5, 1950

"We hold upon this earth the place of God Almighty."

- Pope Leo XIII, in an Encyclical Letter, dated June 20, 1894

Not the Creator of the Universe, In Genesis 2:1-3, - but the Catholic Church "can claim the honor of having granted man a pause to his work every seven days."   *- S.D. Mosna, "Storia della Domenica," 1969, pp. 366-367*

"CATHOLICISM SPEAKS"

"The Pope is not only the representative of Jesus Christ, but he is Jesus Christ Himself, hidden under veil of flesh."

- "The Catholic National," July 1895

"If Protestants would follow the Bible, they should worship God on the Sabbath Day. In keeping the Sunday they are following a law of the Catholic Church."

- Albert Smith, Chancellor of the Archdiocese of Baltimore, replying for the Cardinal, in a letter dated February 10, 1920

"We define that the Holy Apostolic See (the Vatican) and the Roman Pontiff holds the primacy over the whole world."

- A Decree of the Council of Trent, quoted in Philippe Labbe and Gabriel Cossart, "The Most Holy Councils," Vol. 13, col. 1167

"It was the Catholic Church which, by the authority of Jesus Christ, has transferred this rest (from the Bible Sabbath) to the Sunday . . . Thus the observance of Sunday by the Protestants is an homage they pay, in spite of themselves, to the authority of the (Catholic) Church."

- Monsignor Louis Segur, "Plain Talk about the Protestantism of Today," p. 213

"We observe Sunday instead of Saturday because the Catholic Church transferred the solemnity from Saturday to Sunday."

- Peter Geiermann, CSSR, "A Doctrinal Catechism," 1957 edition, p. 50

"We Catholics, then, have precisely the same authority for keeping Sunday holy instead of Saturday as we have for every other article of our creed, namely, the authority of the Church . . . whereas you who are Protestants have really no authority for it whatever; for there is no authority for it (Sunday sacredness) in the Bible, and you will not allow that there can be authority for it anywhere else. Both you and we do, in fact, follow tradition in this matter; but we follow it, believing it to be a part of God's word, and the (Catholic) Church to be its divinely appointed guardian and interpreter; you follow it (the Catholic Church), denouncing it all the time as a fallible and treacherous guide, which often 'makes the commandments of God of none effect' quoting Matthew 15:6."

- The Brotherhood of St. Paul, "The Clifton Tracts," Vol 4, tract 4, p. 15

"The Church changed the observance of the Sabbath to Sunday by right of the divine, infallible authority given to her by her founder, Jesus Christ. The Protestant claiming the Bible to be the only guide of faith, has no warrant for observing Sunday. In this matter the Seventh-day Adventist is the only consistent Protestant."

- "The Catholic Universe Bulletin," August 14, 1942, p. 4

The Bible is our only safe guide

"PROTESTANTISM SPEAKS"

Baptist: "There was and is a command to keep holy the Sabbath day, but that Sabbath day was not Sunday. It will however be readily said, and with some show of triumph, that the Sabbath was transferred from the seventh to the first day of the week, with all its duties, privileges and sanctions. Earnestly desiring information on this subject, which I have studied for many years, I ask, where can the record of such a transaction be found? Not in the New Testament - absolutely not. There is no scriptural evidence of the change of the Sabbath institution from the seventh to the first day of the week."

- Dr. E.T. Hiscox, author of the "Baptist Manual"

Congregationalist: "It is quite clear that however rigidly or devotedly we may spend Sunday, we are not keeping the Sabbath. . . The Sabbath was founded on specific, divine command. We can plead no such command for the observance of Sunday. . . There is not a single line in the New Testament to suggest that we incur any penalty by violating the supposed sanctity of Sunday."

- Dr. R. W. Dale, "The Ten Commandments," p. 106-107

Lutheran Free Church: "For when there could not be produced one solitary place in the Holy Scriptures which testified that either the Lord Himself or the apostles had ordered such a transfer of the Sabbath to Sunday, then it was not easy to answer the question: Who has transferred the Sabbath, and who has had the right to do it?"   *- George Sverdrup, "A New Day"*

Protestant Episcopal: "The day is now changed from the seventh to the first day . . . but as we meet with no Scriptural direction for the change, we may conclude it was done by the authority of the church."

- "Explanation of Catechism"

Baptist: "The Scriptures nowhere call the first day of the week the Sabbath . . . There is no Scriptural authority for so doing, nor of course, any Scriptural obligation."   *-"The Watchman"*

Presbyterian: "There is no word, no hint in the New Testament about abstaining from work on Sunday. The observance of Ash Wednesday, or Lent, stands exactly on the same footing as the observance of Sunday. Into the rest of Sunday no Divine Law enters."   *- Canon Eyton, in "The Ten Commandments"*

Anglican: "And where are we told in the Scriptures that we are to keep the first day at all? We are commanded to keep the seventh; but we are nowhere commanded to keep the first day."

- Isaac Williams, "Plain Sermons on the Catechism," pp. 334, 336

Disciples of Christ: "There is no direct Scriptural authority for designating the first day 'the Lord's Day.'" *-" Dr. D.H. Lucas, "Christian Oracle," January, 1890*

"PROTESTANTISM SPEAKS"

Methodist: "It is true that there is no positive command for infant baptism. Nor is there any for keeping holy the first day of the week. Many believe that Christ changed the Sabbath. But, from His own words, we see that He came for no such purpose. Those who believe that Jesus changed the Sabbath base it only on a supposition." — *Amos Binney, "Theological Compendium," pp. 180-181*

Episcopalian: "We have made the change from the seventh day to the first day, from Saturday to Sunday, on the authority of the one holy, catholic, apostolic church of Christ." — *Bishop Symour, "Why We keep Sunday"*

Southern Baptist: "The sacred name of the Seventh day is Sabbath. This fact is too clear to require argument (Exodus 20:10 quoted) . . . On this point the plain teaching of the Word has been admitted in all ages . . . Not once did the disciples apply the Sabbath law to the first day of the week - that folly was left for a later age, nor did they pretend that the first day supplanted the seventh." — *Joseph Judson Taylor, "The Sabbath Question," pp. 14-17, 41*

American Congregationalist: "The current notion that Christ and His apostles authoritatively substituted the first day for the seventh, is absolutely without any authority in the New Testament." — *Dr. Layman Abbot, in the "Christian Union," June 26, 1890*

Christian Church: "Now there is no testimony in all the oracles of heaven that the Sabbath is changed, or that the Lord's Day came in the room of it." — *Alexander Campbell, in "The Reporter," October 8, 1921*

Baptist: "To me it seems unaccountable that Jesus, during three years' discussion with His disciples, often conversing with them upon the Sabbath question, discussing it in some of its various aspects, freeing it from its false (Jewish traditional) glosses, never alluded to any transference of the day; also, that during the forty days of His resurrection life, no such thing was intimated. Nor, so far as we know, did the Spirit, which was given to bring to their remembrance all things whatsoever that He had said unto them, deal with this question. Nor yet did the inspired apostles, in preaching the gospel, founding churches, counseling and instructing those founded, discuss or approach the subject.

"Of course I quite well know that Sunday did come into use in early Christian history as a religious day, as we learn from the Christian Fathers and other sources. But what a pity that it comes branded with the mark of Paganism, and christened with the name of the sun-god, then adopted and sanctified by the Papal apostasy, and bequeathed as a sacred legacy to Protestantism." — *Dr. E.T. Hiscox, report of his sermon at the Baptist Minister's Convention, in "New York Examiner," November 16, 1893*

Sunday sacredness is not commanded or practiced in the Bible

"You may read the Bible from Genesis to Revelation, and you will not find a single line authorizing the sanctification of Sunday. The Scriptures enforce the religious observance of Saturday, a day which we (Catholics) never sanctify."

Cardinal Gibbons, The Faith of Our Fathers, page 111.

Think it through:

"Howbeit *in vain do they worship me, teaching for doctrines the commandments of men.* For laying aside the commandment of God, ye hold the tradition of men, as the washing of pots and cups: and many other such like things ye do. *And he said unto them, Full well ye reject the commandment of God, that ye may keep your own tradition.*"   Mark 7:7-9

WHY BAPTISM?

Note: The English word baptize is from the Greek "baptizo," meaning "to immerse." In the Bible, "to bury beneath the water."

According to Jesus, how important is baptism?

"Jesus answered, Verily, verily, I say unto thee, *Except a man be born of water and of the spirit, he cannot enter into the kingdom of God.*"
John 3:5

"*He that believeth and is baptized shall be saved.*"
Mark 16:16

Who was first to administer baptism in the New Testament?

"*In those days came John the Baptist, preaching in the wilderness of Judea,* And saying, Repent ye: for the kingdom of heaven is at hand . . . . Then went out to him Jerusalem, and all Judea, and all the region round about Jordan, *And were baptized of him in Jordan, confessing their sins.*"
Matthew 3:1-6

Why was John baptizing in the wilderness?

"*And John also was baptizing in Aenon near to Salim, because there was much water there:* and they came, and were baptized."
John 3:23

Note: John needed "much water" to baptize.   The practice of sprinkling or pouring for baptism crept into the church during the twelfth century A.D.   History preserves this record: "For several centuries after the establishment of Christianity, baptism was usually conferred by immersion; but since the twelfth century, the practice of baptism by infusion (pouring) has prevailed in the Catholic Church, as this manner is attended with less inconvenience than baptism by immersion.   The Church exercises her discretion in adapting the most convenient modes, according to the circumstances of time and place." James Cardinal Gibbons, *Faith of Our Fathers*, 94th edition, pg. 277 (emphasis supplied).

How do we know that Jesus was baptized by immersion?

"And straightway *coming up out of the water*, he saw the heavens opened, and the Spirit like a dove descending upon him."   Mark 1:10

Why was it necessary for Jesus to be baptized?

"Then cometh Jesus from Galilee to Jordan unto John, to be baptized of him.   But John forbade him, saying, I have need to be baptized of thee, and comest thou to me? *And Jesus answering said unto him, Suffer it to be so now: for thus it becometh us to fulfil all righteousness."*
Matthew 3:13-15

Note: "Jesus did not receive baptism as a confession of guilt on His own account.   He identified Himself with sinners, taking the steps that we are to take, and doing the work that we must do.   His life of suffering and patient endurance after His baptism was also an example to us." E. G. White, *The Desire of Ages*, pg. 111.

Bible Conditions For Baptism:

1. "Then Peter said unto them, *Repent, and be baptized* every one of you in the name of Jesus Christ for the remission of sins, and ye shall receive the gift of the Holy Ghost." Acts 2:38

2. "And the eunuch answered Philip, and said .... *what doth hinder me to be baptized?* And Philip said, *If thou believest with all thine heart, thou mayest.* And he answered and said, I believe that Jesus Christ is the Son of God." Acts 8:34-37

3. *"Go ye therefore, and teach* all nations, *baptizing them* in the name of the Father, and of the Son, and of the Holy Ghost: *Teaching them to observe all things whatsoever I have commanded you."* Matthew 28:19, 20

Peter preached Jesus as "Christ" on the Day of Pentecost. How did the people respond?

"Then *they that gladly received his word were baptized:* and the same day there were added unto them about three thousand souls." Acts 2:41

What instruction was given to Paul after he understood the Plan of Salvation?

"And now why tarriest thou? *arise, and be baptized, and wash away thy sins,* calling on the name of the Lord." Acts 22:16

What spiritual lessons are experienced in baptism?

"Know ye not, that so many of us as were baptized into Jesus Christ *were baptized into his death?* Therefore we are buried with him by baptism into death: that like as Christ was raised up from the dead by the glory of the Father, even so we also should walk in newness of life. For if we have been planted together in the likeness of his death, *we shall be also in the likeness of his resurrection:* Knowing this, that our old man is crucified with him, that the body of sin might be destroyed, that henceforth we should not serve sin."

Romans 6:3-6

Note: By baptism we declare our faith in our Savior's death, burial, and resurrection. Being baptized into His death, we die to our sins. Being buried with Him by baptism, we bury our past sinful life. Finally, we are raised to new spiritual life "in the likeness of His resurrection."

Thought Promises:

"For as many of you *as have been baptized* into Christ have put on Christ."   Galatians 3:27

"Now unto him that is able to keep you from falling, and to present you faultless before the presence of his glory with exceeding joy, to the only wise God our Saviour, be glory and majesty, dominion and power, both now and ever."   Jude 24, 25

WHAT HAPPENS AT DEATH

For what good reason did Jesus reprove the Sadducees and teachers of His day?

"Jesus answered and said unto them, *Ye do err, not knowing the scriptures,* nor the power of God."

Matthew 22:29

Then, if we want to know the truth about the subject of death, to what reliable source should we turn?

"And when they shall say unto you, Seek unto them that have familiar spirits, and unto wizards that peep, and that mutter: *should not a people seek unto their God?* for the living to the dead? *To the law and to the testimony: if they speak not according to this word, it is because there is no light in them.*"

Isaiah 8:19, 20

What does the Bible say happens to a man at death?

"*Then shall the dust return to earth as it was: and the spirit shall return unto God* who gave it."

Ecclesiastes 12:7

This simple statement of Scripture agrees fully with the Genesis record. At man's creation, what two elements did God combine to make man a living soul?

173

"And *the Lord God formed man of the dust
of the ground, and breathed into his nostrils
the breath of life; and man became a living
soul."*   Genesis 2:7

*Note: Here are the same two elements mentioned in
Ecclesiastes 12:7. The "dust of the ground" is the body,
and the "breath of life" is the "spirit" that comes from
God. God did not put a living soul in Adam! Adam
became a living soul after God breathed into his nostrils
the breath of life. A light bulb cannot turn on without
electricity. The light turns on only when the light bulb
and electricity unite. When the electricity is turned off,
the light ceases to exist. According to the Bible, when
the breath departs from the body, the soul ceases to exist.
Here is the simple equation:*

DUST + SPIRIT = LIVING SOUL

DUST − SPIRIT = DEAD PERSON

Can we be sure that the Scripture expressions "breath of life" and "spirit" mean the same?

"All the while my *breath* is in me, and the *spirit*
of God is in my nostrils."   Job 27:3

Note: Here is the equation once more:

DUST + BREATH (or Spirit) = LIVING SOUL

DUST − BREATH (or Spirit) = DEAD SOUL

What the Bible Says About Man's Condition in Death

He has no thought:

"His breath goeth forth, he returneth to his earth; *in that very day his thoughts perish.*"   Psalm 146:4

He has no knowledge:

"For the living know that they shall die: but *the dead know not any thing,* neither have they any more a reward; for the memory of them is forgotten."

Ecclesiastes 9:5

He has no emotion:

"Also *their love, and their hatred, and their envy, is now perished;* neither have they any more a portion for ever in any thing that is done under the sun."

Ecclesiastes 9:6

There is no activity:

"Whatsoever thy hand findeth to do, do it with thy might; *for there is no work, nor device, nor knowledge, nor wisdom, in the grave,* whither thou goest."   Ecclesiastes 9:10

He does not praise God:

"*The dead praise not the Lord,* neither any that go down into silence."   Psalm 115:17

"For *in death there is no remembrance of thee: in the grave who shall give thee thanks?*"

Psalm 6:5

How did Jesus explain "death" to His disciples?

"Our friend Lazarus sleepeth; but I go, that I may awake him out of sleep. Then said his disciples, Lord, if he sleep, he shall do well. Howbeit Jesus spake of his death: but they thought that he had spoken of taking of rest in sleep. *Then said Jesus unto them plainly, Lazarus is dead."*

John 11:11-14

When did Martha expect her brother, Lazarus, to live again?

"Jesus saith unto her, Thy brother shall rise again. Martha saith unto him, *I know that he shall rise again in the resurrection at the last day."*

John 11:23, 24

Note: Martha was a close friend and follower of Jesus. She had listened attentively to what He taught about death, and she believed that the dead would be raised in the Resurrection at the last day as Christ promised.

When can we expect the resurrection of all those who have died believing in Jesus?

"For as in Adam all die, even so in Christ shall all be made alive. But every man in his own order: Christ the firstfruits; *afterward they that are Christ's at his coming."*   1 Corinthians 15:22, 23

According to the Bible, whose voice will the dead hear before their resurrection?

"Marvel not at this: for *the hour is coming, in*

the which all that are in the graves shall hear his voice, And shall come forth; they that have done good, unto the resurrection of life; and they that have done evil, unto the resurrection of damnation."

John 5:28, 29

According to Paul, when are the saints resurrected and taken to heaven?

"For the Lord himself shall descend from heaven with a shout, with the voice of the archangel, and with the trump of God: *and the dead in Christ shall rise first: Then we which are alive and remain shall be caught up together with them in the clouds, to meet the Lord in the air:* and so shall we ever be with the Lord."

1 Thessalonians 4:16, 17

At the resurrection, how will our bodies be changed?

"For our conversation is in heaven; from whence also we look for the Saviour, the Lord Jesus Christ: *Who shall change our vile body, that it may be fashioned like unto his glorious body,* according to the working whereby he is able even to subdue all things unto himself."

Philippians 3:20, 21

After His resurrection, Jesus appeared to His disciples. Did He, as many suppose, have a "spirit body"?

"Jesus himself stood in the midst of them, and saith unto them, Peace be unto you. But they were terrified and affrighted, and supposed that they had seen a spirit. And he said unto them, Why are ye troubled? and why do thoughts arise in your hearts? Behold my hands and my feet, that it is I myself: *handle me, and see; for a spirit hath not flesh and bones, as ye see me have."*   Luke 24:36-39

Note: Even though the resurrected body of Jesus was made up of "flesh and bones," the disciples still did not believe Him. "and while they yet believed not for joy, and wondered, he said unto them, Have ye here any meat? And they gave him a piece of a broiled fish, and of a honeycomb. And he took it, and did eat before them." Luke 24:41-43

Thought Promises:

"I am he that liveth, and was dead; and, behold, I am alive for evermore, Amen; and have the keys of hell and of death."   Revelation 1:18

"Behold, I shew you a mystery; We shall not all sleep, but we shall all be changed, In a moment, in the twinkling of an eye, at the last trump: *for the trumpet shall sound, and the dead shall be raised incorruptible, and we shall be changed.* For this corruptible must put on incorruption, and this mortal must put on immortality. So when this corruptible shall have put on incorruption, and this mortal shall have put on immortality, then shall be brought to pass the saying that is written, Death is swallowed up in victory. O death, where is thy sting? O grave, where is thy victory?"
1 Corinthians 15:51-55

1,000 YEARS OF PEACE

Note: The phrase "one thousand years" appears six times in Revelation Chapter 20. This "one thousand year" period is often referred to as the millennium from the Latin mille and annus, meaning one thousand years.

How many resurrections did Jesus say would take place?

"Marvel not at this: for the hour is coming, in the which all that are in the graves shall hear his voice, And shall come forth; they that have done good, unto *the resurrection of life*; and they that have done evil, unto *the resurrection of damnation.*" John 5:28, 29

When will the resurrection of the righteous dead take place?

"For the Lord himself shall descend from heaven with a shout, with the voice of the archangel, and with the trump of God: *and the dead in Christ shall rise first."* 1 Thessalonians 4:16

Note: It is at the Second Coming of Jesus that the resurrection of the righteous takes place.

What does the book of Revelation call this resurrection of the righteous?

"Blessed and holy is he that hath part in *the first resurrection*: on such the second death hath no power, but they shall be priests of God and of Christ, and shall reign with him a thousand years." Revelation 20:6

179

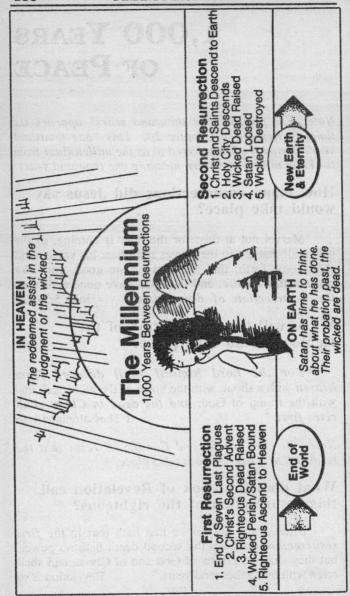

IN HEAVEN
The redeemed assist in the judgment of the wicked.

The Millennium
1,000 Years Between Resurrections

First Resurrection
1. End of Seven Last Plagues
2. Christ's Second Advent
3. Righteous Dead Raised
4. Wicked Perish/Satan Bound
5. Righteous Ascend to Heaven

Second Resurrection
1. Christ and Saints Descend to Earth
2. Holy City Descends
3. Wicked Dead Raised
4. Satan Loosed
5. Wicked Destroyed

New Earth & Eternity

ON EARTH
Satan has time to think about what he has done. Their probation past, the wicked are dead.

End of World

The Biblical Millennium

We live in the last days of history. The end of life as men now know it is nearly ended. Soon Jesus will return. We only have one period of probation—and that is during our present life. *The Millennium will not be a thousand years of glory and peace here on earth!* And it will not be an age of technological progress or a "second chance" for the wicked. *All mankind will not be converted before it, during it, or after it!* And neither Christ nor His redeemed ones will be on the earth during that thousand years.

Here is the truth about the Millennium and the events that mark its beginning and end:

1-Jesus is going to return for His people: He promised us that He would (John 14:1-3), and so we can know that He will.

2-There are four identifying marks of His Second Advent that cannot be counterfeited by false Christs: **(1)** He will come so that all alive on the earth at that time can see Him return (Rev 1:7; Ac 1:9; Matt 24:30, 23-27). **(2)** He will come so all can hear Him as He returns (Matt 24:31; 1 Thess 4:16). **(3)** He will come in majestic glory—His own glory, His Father's glory, and the glory of millions of angels that will come with Him (Lk 9:26; Matt 25:2-4; Matt 25:31; Rev 6:14-17). **(4)** He will come unexpectedly (Matt 24:44; 24:36).

3-His Second coming will mark the beginning of the Millennium. Six events will take place: **(1)** He will raise the righteous dead (1 Thess 4:16). **(2)** He will catch up the righteous living together with the resurrected righteous dead—to meet Him in the clouds (1 Thess 4:17). **(3)** He will change their vile bodies to be like unto His glorious body (Phil 3:20-21) and translate them (1 Cor 15:51-55; Isa 25:9). **(4)** Having gathered all the righteous (1 Thess 4:17-18; Matt 25:34-40; 24:30, 31), He will take His redeemed ones to heaven (Jn 14:1-3; 17:24; 1 Thess 4:16-18). **(5)** He will destroy the living wicked with the brightness of His coming (Lk 17:26-30; 2 Thess 2:8). **(6)** He will bind Satan to this earth for 1,000 years (Rev 20:2-3).

4-During the Millennium, the earth will be desolate (Rev 20:3; Jer 4:23-26; Isa 24:1,3). The wicked are dead (2 Thess 2:8). There is no man left (Isa 24:20-22; Jer 4:25,26; 25:31-33). Satan is bound on a desolate earth (Rev 20:1-3). The righteous are in heaven (Rev 20:4,6; Dan 7:22) engaged in a work of judgment (Rev 20:4; 1 Cor 6:1-3; Acts 24:25; Jude 6).

5-At the close of the Millenium, the Holy City descends from heaven (Rev 20:9; 21:1-5; Zech 14:4,9); the wicked are raised in the "second resurrection" (Rev 20:5, first part). Satan is thus loosed to deceive them again (Rev 20:7-8). Satan and the wicked surround the Holy City to take it (Rev 20:8-9). All of the wicked are destroyed (Rev 20:9), and this earth is made new (Rev 21:1-5; 2 Pet 3:10-14).

What happens to the "living righteous" when Jesus comes?

"Then we which are alive and remain shall be caught up together with them in the clouds, to meet the Lord in the air: and so shall we ever be with the Lord."   1 Thessalonians 4:17

What happens to the "living wicked" when Jesus comes?

Old Testament Prophecy:

"And the slain of the Lord shall be at that day from one end of the earth even unto the other end of the earth: they shall not be lamented, neither gathered, nor buried; *they shall be dung upon the ground."*   Jeremiah 25:33

New Testament Prophecy:

"And then shall that Wicked be revealed, whom the Lord shall consume with the spirit of his mouth, *and shall destroy with the brightness of his coming."*   2 Thessalonians 2:8

How do we know the "wicked dead" (*the un-saved of ages past*) will not be disturbed or resurrected at the Second Coming of Jesus?

"But the rest of the dead lived not again until the thousand years were finished."
                                    Revelation 20:5

Note: The 1,000 year period of peace begins immediately following the Second Coming of Jesus. These 1,000 years are bounded by two resurrections: 1) the resurrection of the righteous which occurs at the beginning of the 1,000 years when Jesus comes again, and 2) the resurrection of the wicked which occurs at the end of the 1,000 years. Examine the chart carefully that accompanies this study. It will simplify these Bible events.

What will the righteous (*the redeemed of all ages*) be doing in heaven during the 1,000 years?

"And I saw thrones, and they sat upon them, and judgment was given unto them: and I saw the souls of them that were beheaded for the witness of Jesus, and for the word of God, and which had not worshipped the beast, neither his image, neither had received his mark upon their foreheads, or in their hands; *and they lived and reigned with Christ a thousand years* . . . . . Blessed and holy is he that hath part in the first resurrection: on such the second death hath no power, but *they shall be priests of God and of Christ, and shall reign with him a thousand years."*   Revelation 20:4, 6

"Do ye not know that *the saints shall judge the world?"*   1 Corinthians 6:2

What will be the condition of the earth during the 1,000 years?

Old Testament Prophecy:

"I beheld the earth, and, lo, it was without form, and void; and the heavens, and they had no light. I beheld the mountains, and, lo, they trembled, and all the hills moved lightly. *I beheld, and lo, there was no man*, and all the birds of the heavens were fled. *I beheld, and, lo, the fruitful place was a wilderness, and all the cities thereof were broken down at the presence of the Lord, and by his fierce anger. For thus hath the Lord said, The whole land shall be desolate; yet will I not make a full end."*   Jeremiah 4:23-27

New Testament Prophecy:

"And the seventh angel poured out his vial into the air; and there came a great voice out of the temple of heaven, from the throne, saying, It is done. And there were voices, and thunders, and lightnings; *and there was a great earthquake, such as was not since men were upon the earth, so mighty an earthquake, and so great. . . . . and the cities of the nations fell. . . . And every island fled away, and the mountains were not found."*
                                      Revelation 16:17-20

What happens to Satan during the 1,000 years?

"And I saw an angel come down from heaven, having the key of the bottomless pit and a great chain in his hand. *And he laid hold on the dragon, that old serpent, which is the Devil, and Satan, and bound him a thousand years, And cast him into the bottomless pit, and shut him up, and set a seal upon him, that he should deceive the nations no more, till the thousand years should be fulfilled: and after that he must be loosed a little season."*   Revelation 20:1-3

Note: "For a thousand years, Satan will wander to and fro in the desolate earth to behold the results of his rebellion against the Law of God. During this time his *sufferings are intense. Since his fall, his life of unceasing activity has banished reflection; but he is now deprived of his power and left to contemplate the part which he has acted since first he rebelled against the government of heaven, and to look forward with trembling and terror to the dreadful future when he must suffer for all the evil that he has done and be punished for the sins that he has caused to be committed." The Great Controversy, pg. 660.*

When will the second resurrection (for the wicked) take place?

"But the rest of the dead lived not again until the thousand years were finished."

Revelation 20:5

When will Satan be released from his prison?

"And when the thousand years are expired, Satan shall be loosed out of his prison."

Revelation 20:7

When Satan is released, what act will reveal that he has not changed but remains a rebel against God?

"And when the thousand years are expired, Satan shall be loosed out of his prison, And shall go out to deceive the nations which are in the four quarters of the earth, God and Magog, to gather them together to battle: the number of whom is as the sand of the sea." Revelation 20:7, 8

What will happen to Satan and his resurrected, wicked followers, as they attempt to take the City of God?

"And they went up on the breadth of the earth, and compassed the camp of the saints about, and the beloved city: and fire came down from God out of heaven, and devoured them. . . . And death and hell were cast into the lake of fire. *This is the second death. And whosoever was not found written in the book of life was cast into the lake of fire."* Revelation 20:9, 14, 15

When the fire from God has completed its cleansing work, what has God promised to do for the redeemed?

"Nevertheless we, according to his promise, look for new heavens and a new earth, wherein dwelleth righteousness."

2 Peter 3:13

Who will inhabit the earth made new?

"Blessed are the meek: for they shall inherit the earth."   Matthew 5:5

Thought Promise:

"And I heard a great voice out of heaven saying, Behold, the tabernacle of God is with men, and he will dwell with them, and they shall be his people, and God himself shall be with them, and be their God. *And God shall wipe away all tears from their eyes; and there shall be no more death, neither sorrow, nor crying, neither shall there be any more pain: for the former things are passed away.* And he that sat upon the throne said, Behold, I make all things new. And he said unto me, *Write: for these words are true and faithful."*   Revelation 21:3-5

WHAT AND WHERE IS HELL

When will a "harvest", or separation between the wicked and the righteous take place?

"The enemy that sowed them is the devil, *the harvest is the end of the world*; and the reapers are the angels. As therefore the tares are gathered and burned in the fire: *so shall it be in the end of this world*."
Matthew 13: 39,40

Can we be certain that *no person,* righteous or wicked, has received any reward or punishment before the Second Coming of Jesus?

"For the Son of man shall come in the glory of his Father with his angels; *and then he shall reward every man according to his works*."

Matthew 16:27

Note: Bible statements regarding the judgment and punishment of the wicked and the eternal reward of the righteous are numerous and clear. They plainly reveal that the wicked are not now "burning in hell" nor yet have the righteous received their reward! Notice these typical scripture declarations:

"The Lord knoweth how to deliver the godly out of temptations, *and to reserve the unjust unto the day of judgment to be punished:*"   2 Peter 2:9

"And, behold, I come quickly; and *my reward is with me, to give every man* according as his work shall be."   Revelation 22:12

Will God find pleasure in the death of the wicked?

"Say unto them, *As I live, saith the Lord God, I have no pleasure in the death of the wicked; but that the wicked turn from his way and live:* turn ye, turn ye from your evil ways; for why will ye die. . .?"   Ezekiel 33:11

Is it God's plan that any man or woman should perish?

"The Lord is not slack concerning his promise, as some count slackness, but is longsuffering toward us, *not willing that any should perish, but that all should come to repentance.*"   2 Peter 3:9 (New King James)

For whom will God prepare the final fire of judgment?

New Testament Prophecy:

"Then shall he say also unto them on the left hand, Depart from me, ye cursed, into everlasting fire, *prepared for the devil and his angels.*"   Matthew 25:41

Old Testament Prophecy:

"Thou hast defiled thy sanctuaries by the multitude of thine iniquities, by the iniquity of thy traffic; *therefore will I bring forth a fire from the midst of thee, it shall devour thee, and I will bring thee to ashes upon the earth in the sight of all them that behold thee.*"   Ezekiel 28:18

How utterly complete will be the destruction of Satan and those wicked who have refused salvation?

Of Satan:

"All they that know thee among the people shall be astonished at thee: thou shalt be a terror, *and never shalt thou be any more.*" Ezekiel 28:19

Of The Wicked:

"*For, behold, the day cometh, that shall burn as an oven; and all the proud, yea, and all that do wickedly, shall be stubble: and the day that cometh shall burn them up,* saith the Lord of hosts, that it shall leave them neither root nor branch."

Malachi 4:1

Note: See how plainly the Bible describes the utter destruction of the wicked:

a. "The Lord preserveth all them that love him: *but all the wicked will he destroy.*" Psalm 145:20

b. "The wicked shall perish . . . *they shall consume; into smoke shall they consume away.*"

Psalm 37:20

c. "The Lord shall swallow them up in his wrath, and *the fire shall devour them.*" Psalm 21:9

d. "*They shall be as though they had not been.*" Obadiah 16

After the destruction of the wicked is completed, how much fire will remain?

"Behold, they shall be as stubble; the fire shall burn them; they shall not deliver themselves from the power of the flame: *there shall not be a coal to warm at, nor fire to sit before it.*"　　　Isaiah 47:14

What does the Bible call the death that is the final punishment of the wicked?

"The fearful, and unbelieving, and the abominable, and murderers, and whoremongers, and sorcerers, and idolaters, and all liars, shall have their part in the lake which burneth with fire and brimstone: *which is the second death.*"　　　Revelation 21:8

How clearly did Jesus indicate that the "second death" judgment will destroy both body and soul?

"And fear not them which kill the body, but are not able to kill the soul: but *rather fear him which is able to destroy both soul and body in hell.*"
　　　Matthew 10:28

Note: The expression "hell" is actually translated from the original language meaning "grave". While some believe a soul cannot die or be destroyed, the Bible plainly declares, "the soul that sinneth, it shall die." Ezekiel 18:4.

What kind of fire will God use to ultimately cleanse the earth of sin?

"Even as Sodom and Gomorrha, and the cities about them in like manner, giving themselves over to fornication, and going after strange flesh, *are set forth for an example, suffering the vengeance of eternal fire.*"　　　Jude 7

Note: This "eternal" fire is not burning today! It is the effect of the fire, that is eternal, and not the fire itself.

Is there another example of "eternal" or "unquenchable" fire in the Bible?

"But if ye will not hearken unto me to hallow the Sabbath day, and not to bear a burden, even entering in at the gates of Jerusalem on the Sabbath day; *then will I kindle a fire in the gates thereof, and it shall devour the palaces of Jerusalem, and it shall not be quenched.*"   Jeremiah 17:27

Note: Ancient Jerusalem was burned with a fire that could not be quenched (Jeremiah 52:12, 13). It burned the city to the ground, but it is not burning today!

Doesn't the Bible contradict itself? Doesn't the Bible speak of Judgment fire that burns for ever and ever?

"And the devil that deceived them was *cast into the lake of fire* and brimstone, where the beast and the false prophet are, *and shall be tormented day and night for ever and ever.*"   Revelation 20:10

Note: At first glance it may appear that the Bible is contradicting itself. But Scripture must be compared with Scripture. For example the previous verse in Revelation (20:9) declares:

"And they went up on the breadth of the earth, and compassed the camp of the saints about, and the beloved city: *and fire came down from God out of heaven, and devoured them.*"   Revelation 20:9

Note: "Fire from God devours them"! God does not burn human beings for millions of years because they lived wickedly for 60, 70 or 80 years here on earth. This is not consistent with God's love or character or the whole of Scripture on the subject. The results of the fire are eternal not the fire itself!

Are there other examples of "for ever" used in Scripture that can clarify this matter?

a. "His master shall bore his ear through with an awl; *and he shall serve him for ever.*" Exodus 21:6

Note: "for ever" must necessarily mean for as long as the servant remained alive.

b. "But Hannah went not up; for she said unto her husband, I will not go up until the child be weaned, and then I will bring him, *that he may appear before the Lord, and there abide for ever* . . . For this child I prayed; and the Lord hath given me my petition which I asked of him: Therefore also I have lent him to the Lord; *as long as he liveth he shall be lent to the Lord.*"

1 Samuel 1:22, 27, 28

God's Promise To The Righteous:

"And God shall wipe away all tears from their eyes; and there shall be no more death, neither sorrow, nor crying, neither shall there be any more pain: *for the former things are passed away."*

Revelation 21:4

THE BIBLE AND GOOD HEALTH

What is God's wish for everyone?

"Beloved, *I wish above all things that thou mayest prosper and be in health.*" 3 John 2

What has God promised to do for His people if they will obey Him?

"And ye shall serve the Lord your God, and He shall bless thy bread, and thy water; and *I will take sickness away from the midst of thee.*"

Exodus 23:25

As our creator, what does God claim as His property?

"What? *know ye not that your body is the temple of the Holy Ghost* which is in you, which ye have of God, *and ye are not your own?* For ye are bought with a price: therefore glorify God in your body, and in your spirit, which are God's."

1 Corinthians 6:19, 20

What warning has God issued regarding the care of the body?

"Know ye not that ye are the temple of God, and that the Spirit of God dwelleth in you? *If any man defile the temple of God him shall God destroy: for the temple of God is holy, which temple ye are.*"

1 Corinthians 3:16, 17

Note: The Christian should avoid any and all harmful substances. Tobacco contains nicotine, a deadly poison. Recent scientific findings establish the fact that the use of tobacco often shortens the life span by as much as one-third. This violates God's commandment against killing (Exodus 20:13). Most people are aware of the harmful effects of tobacco, but what about debilitating beverages? "Tests clearly showed that the pharmacologic effects of coffee were due to its caffeine content . . . . It is reasonable to classify the coffee-drinking, or caffeine habit with the other drug habits – opiates, alcohol, barbiturates, and nicotine. . . . The popular cola drinks get their appeal from their caffeine content; should not "cola" addiction be classed with drug addiction? There are tea addicts, too." New England Medical Journal, May 13, 1954.

What is man's reasonable service toward God?

"I beseech you therefore, brethren, by the mercies of God, that ye *present your bodies a living sacrifice, holy, acceptable unto God, which is your reasonable service."*   Romans 12:1

Note: God wants us to be healthy. In the Bible we find His guidelines for health and happiness. God will not force us to follow His manual, but failure to follow it will result in poor health. His promise is, " If thou wilt diligently hearken to the voice of the Lord thy God, and wilt do that which is right in his sight, and wilt give ear to his commandments, and keep all his statutes, I will put none of these diseases upon thee, which I have brought upon the Egyptians: for I am the Lord that healeth thee. " Exodus 15:26.

Does the Bible advise against the use of alcoholic beverages?

a. "Wine is a mocker, strong drink is raging: and *whosoever is deceived thereby is not wise.*"
Proverbs 20:1

b. "Look not thou upon the wine when it is red, when it giveth his color in the cup, when it moveth itself aright. *At the last it biteth like a serpent, and stingeth like an adder.*" Proverbs 23:31, 32

c. "Nor thieves . . . *nor drunkards. . . shall inherit the kingdom of God.*" 1 Corinthians 6:10

What was God's original plan for man's diet?

"Behold, *I have given you every plant yielding seed* that is on the surface of all the earth, *and every tree which has fruit yielding seed; it shall be food for you.*"
Genesis 1:29 *(New American Standard Version)*

Note: God's original diet for man included grains, nuts, fruits and herbs (vegetables). Flesh food was not included in man's diet until after the flood (Genesis 9:1-3). When flesh foods became part of man's diet, his life span was greatly shortened!

What distinction or division did God make between the animals when He sent them into Noah's ark?

"*Of every clean beast thou shalt take to thee by sevens,* the male and his female: and of *beasts that are not clean by two,* the male and his female."
Genesis 7:2

What is God's definition of a "clean" animal?

"And the Lord spake unto Moses and to Aaron, saying unto them, Speak unto the children of Israel, saying, *These are the beasts which ye shall eat among all the beasts that are on the earth. Whatsoever parteth the hoof, and is clovenfooted, and cheweth the cud, among the beasts, that shall ye eat.*"   Leviticus 11:1-3

What are some of the animals God lists as "unclean" and unfit for food?

"However, of those that chew the cud or that have a split hoof completely divided *you may not eat the camel, the rabbit or the coney. Although they chew the cud, they do not have a split hoof;* they are ceremonially unclean for you. *The pig is also unclean; although it has a split hoof, it does not chew the cud. You are not to eat their meat or touch their carcasses.*"

Deuteronomy 14:7, 8 (*New International Version*)

Note: In other words, animals of the field must pass these two tests. Evidently there is something unwholesome about animals that do not pass these tests or God would not withhold them from us, for "no good thing will he withold from them that walk uprightly." Psalm 84:11.

What about seafood and fish?

"*These shall ye eat of all that are in the waters: whatsoever hath fins and scales in the waters, in the seas, and in the rivers, them shall ye eat. And all that have not fins and scales* in the seas, and in the rivers, of all that move in the waters, and of any living thing which is in the waters, *they shall be an abomination unto you.*"

Leviticus 11:9, 10

Are there "clean" and "unclean" fowl?

"You may eat any clean bird. But these you may not eat: the eagle, the vulture, the black vulture, the red kite, the black kite, any kind of falcon, any kind of raven, the horned owl, the screech owl, the gull, any kind of hawk, the little owl, the great owl, the white owl, the desert owl, the osprey, the cormorant, the stork, any kind of heron, the hoopoe and the bat."

Deuteronomy 14:11-18 (*New International Version*)

Years after Peter became a Christian, he received a vision from God. In his vision, he saw a great sheet descend from heaven filled with unclean animals and heard a voice saying to him, "Rise, Peter; kill, and eat." What did Peter reveal about his diet?

"I have never eaten anything that is common or unclean."

Acts 10:14

Note: Peter did NOT change his diet when he became a Christian. He observed the dietary laws of the Old Testament.

What was not clear to Peter after he had received this strange vision?

"Peter doubted in himself what this vision which he had seen should mean."

Acts 10:17

Two days later, what did Peter finally understand was the meaning of his strange vision?

"God has shown me that *I should not call any man* common or unclean."   Acts 10:28 (NKJV)

Note: In the eyes of a Jew, a Gentile was an unclean human being, and Jews were taught not to associate with Gentiles. This vision was the means God used to convince Peter that it was now time to take the gospel message to the Gentiles.

Some Christians use Chapter 10 of Acts, especially verse 15, "What God hath cleansed, that call not thou common," as license for eating unclean animals. However, a careful reading of the vision reveals that God told Peter not to treat any human being as unclean or common. The human stomach, is the same whether Jew or Gentile! God's dietary laws have never changed.

A Summary Of Bible Principles For Good Health

1. *Eat at regular intervals and avoid eating between meals.* "Eat in due season."
   Ecclesiastes 10:17

2. *Eat to live and don't live to eat.* "Put a knife to thy throat, if thou be a man given to appetite."
   Proverbs 23:2

3. *Rest according to God's plan.* "Six days shalt thou labor, and do all thy work; but the seventh day is the sabbath of the Lord thy God; in it thou shalt not do any work."   Exodus 20:9, 10

   "Come ye yourselves apart . . . and rest awhile."
   Mark 6:31

"It is vain for you to rise up early, to sit up late, to eat the bread of sorrows: for so he giveth his beloved sleep."
Psalms 127:2

4. *Keep your body clean*. "Let us cleanse ourselves from all filthiness of the flesh." 2 Corinthians 7:1

"Be ye clean." Isaiah 52:11

5. *Control yourself*. "Every man that striveth for the mastery is temperate in all things."
1 Corinthians 9:25

"Let your moderation be known unto all men."
Philippians 4:5

6. *Put on a happy face*. "A merry heart doeth good like a medicine." Proverbs 17:22

7. *Do not use animal fat or animal blood in any form*. "It shall be a perpetual statue for your generations throughout all your dwellings that ye eat neither fat nor blood." Leviticus 3:17

8. *Help those who are in need*. "Loose the bands of wickedness . . . undo the heavy burdens . . . deal thy bread to the hungry . . . bring the poor that are cast out to thy house . . . When thou seest the naked . . . cover him . . . *Then . . . thine health shall spring forth speedily*." Isaiah 58:6-8

9. *Trust and obey God*. "My son, attend to my words; incline thine ear unto my sayings . . . . For they are life unto those that find them, and health to all their flesh." Proverbs 4:20, 22

10. *Give God the glory in everything that you do*. "Whether therefore ye eat, or drink, or whatsoever ye do, do all to the glory of God."
1 Corinthians 10:31

WHAT THE BIBLE SAYS ABOUT MONEY

Who alone is the rightful owner of this world and everything in it?

"The earth is the Lord's and the fulness thereof; the world, and they that dwell therein."

Psalm 24:1

What else does God claim?

"For *every beast of the forest is mine*, and the cattle upon a thousand hills." Psalm 50:10

"The silver is mine, and the gold is mine, saith the Lord of hosts." Haggai 2:8

Who gives us the ability to obtain wealth?

"But thou shalt remember the Lord thy God: for it is He that giveth thee power to get wealth, that He may establish His covenant which He sware unto thy fathers, as it is this day."

Deuteronomy 8:18

What great danger do we face as we prosper in material goods?

"Beware that thou forget not the Lord thy God . . . lest when thou hast eaten and art full, and hast built goodly houses . . . and when thy herds and thy flocks multiply, and

thy silver and thy gold is multiplied . . . then thine heart be lifted up and thou forget the Lord thy God . . . and thou say in thine heart, my power and the might of mine hand hath gotten me this wealth."   Deuteronomy 8:11-17

"The *love* of money is the root of all evil."
                                                            1 Timothy 6:10

As God prospers us, what important question should be foremost in our thoughts?

"*What shall I render unto the Lord* for all his benefits toward me?"   Psalm 116:12

God makes man a steward or manager of His goods in the earth. What part of these possessions does God claim arc holy to Him?

"*And all the tithe of the land,* whether of the seed of the land, or of the fruit of the tree, *is the Lord's: it is holy unto the Lord.*"
                                                            Leviticus 27:30

Note: Here is an interesting point. God claims as His, one-seventh of our time and one-tenth of our possessions. Tithe means tenth. God does not need any of our wealth. He is the one who has everything. However, He shares His wealth with us that we may give back to Him, thus keeping open the springs of unselfishness, appreciation, and gratitude toward Him. If we were to keep everything for ourselves, greed would take over with all its tragic consequences.

The "tithing" system has been observed by God's people from the earliest times.

Of Abraham, the scripture says:
"And he gave him tithes of all."   Genesis 14:20

And Jacob vowed to God:
"Of all that thou shalt give me I will surely give the tenth unto thee."   Genesis 28:22

How does God appropriate the tithe?

"*I have given the children of Levi all the tenth* in Israel for an inheritance, *for their service which they serve, even the service of the tabernacle* of the congregation."   Numbers 18:21

Note: The Levites were the priests or full-time ministers of those days.

Is tithe paying a valid New Testament principle as well?

"*Do ye not know that they which minister about holy things live of the things of the temple?* and they which wait at the altar are partakers with the altar? *Even so hath the Lord ordained that they which preach the gospel should live of the gospel.*"   1 Corinthians 9:13, 14

What special blessing does God promise to those that faithfully pay tithe?

"*Bring ye all the tithes into the storehouse*, that there may be meat in mine house, *and prove me now herewith, saith the Lord of hosts if I will not open you the windows of heaven, and pour you out a blessing, that there shall not be room enough to receive it. I will rebuke the devourer for your sakes,* and he shall not destroy the fruits of your ground; neither shall your vine cast her fruit before the time in the field, *saith the Lord of hosts."*

Malachi 3:10, 11

What warning is given regarding those who keep the tithe for their own use?

"Will a man rob God? Yet ye have robbed me. But ye say, Wherein have we robbed thee? *In tithes and offerings. Ye are cursed with a curse: for ye have robbed me,* even this whole nation."

Malachi 3:8, 9

Note: A tenth of all our increase belongs to God. It is His holy tithe, to be used in the work of the ministry and to spread the gospel of Christ. Those who return a faithful tithe to God are not giving offerings. What we give above the tithe is an offering, or gift to God.

Think it through:

Some reason, "I cannot afford to give God tithes and offerings; I can scarcely pay my bills now." But specific Bible promises are made to those who trust God and put Him first!

a. *"So why do you worry about clothing?* Consider the lilies of the field, how they grow: they neither toil nor spin; and yet I say to you that even Solomon in all his glory was not arrayed like one of these. Now if God so clothes the grass of the field, which today is, and tomorrow is thrown into the oven, will He not much more clothe you, O you of little faith? *Therefore do not worry, saying, 'What shall we eat?' or 'What shall we drink?' or 'What shall we wear?' For after*

all these things the Gentiles seek. For your heavenly Father knows that you need all these things. But seek first the kingdom of God and His righteousness, and all these things shall be added to you."
> Matthew 6:28-33 (*New King James Version*)

b. *"Honor the Lord with thy substance, and with the first-fruits of all thine increase: So shall thy barns be filled with plenty,* and thy presses shall burst out with new wine."
> Proverbs 3:9, 10

c. *"Give, and it shall be given unto you;* good measure, pressed down, and shaken together, and running over, shall men give into your bosom. *For with the same measure that ye mete withal it shall be measured to you again."*
> Luke 6:38

d. "I have been young, and now am old; *yet have I not seen the righteous forsaken, nor his seed begging bread."*   Psalm 37:25

SUCCESS IN THE CHRISTIAN WAY

Feed On God's Word

What spiritual food, according to Jesus and Peter, must the believer "eat" if he is to maintain a successful Christian experience?

"But he answered and said, It is written, *Man shall not live by bread alone, but by every word that proceedeth out of the mouth of God.*"

Matthew 4:4

"As newborn babes, *desire the sincere milk of the word, that ye may grow thereby.*"

1 Peter 2:2

Why and how should the Scripture be studied?

"*Study to show thyself approved unto God,* a workman that needeth not to be ashamed, *rightly dividing the word of truth.*"   2 Timothy 2:15

Ask God To Direct Your Life

What assurance belongs to those who pray?

"And this is the confidence that we have in him, that, *if we ask any thing according to his will, he heareth us:* And if we know that he hear us, *whatsoever we ask, we know that we have the petitions that we desired of him.*"

1 John 5:14, 15

What exemplary prayer life is recorded of King David, Daniel the Prophet, and Jesus?

David:

"*Evening, and morning, and at noon, will I pray,* and cry aloud: and he shall hear my voice."

Psalm 55:17

Daniel:

"Now when Daniel knew that the writing was signed, he went into his house; and his windows being open in his chamber toward Jerusalem, *he kneeled upon his knees three times a day, and prayed, and gave thanks before his God,* as he did aforetime."

Daniel 6:10

Jesus:

"And in the morning, *rising up a great while before day, he went out, and departed into a solitary place, and there prayed.*"   Mark 1:35

"And it came to pass in those days, that *he went out into a mountain to pray, and continued all night in prayer to God.*"   Luke 6:12

What conditions are necessary in order for our Heavenly Father to answer our prayers?

1. **Perseverance.** "Praying . . . with all perseverance."

Ephesians 6:18

2. **Faith.** "But let him ask in faith."   James 1:6

3. **We need to forgive others.** "First be reconciled to thy brother, and then come and offer thy gift."
                                               Matthew 5:24

4. **We should not have unconfessed sin in our lives.** "If I regard iniquity in my heart, the Lord will not hear me."   Psalm 66:18

5. **We need to keep God's law.** "He that turneth away his ear from hearing the law, even his prayer shall be an abomination."   Proverbs 28:9

6. **Pray according to God's will.** "If we ask anything according to His will, He heareth us."
                                               1 John 5:14

Respect God's Property

Especially His Time

"*Remember the sabbath day, to keep it holy.* Six days shalt thou labor, and do all thy work: But *the seventh day is the sabbath of the Lord thy God:* in it thou shalt not do any work, thou, nor thy son, nor thy daughter, thy manservant, nor thy maidservant, nor thy cattle, nor thy stranger that is within thy gates: for in six days the Lord made heaven and earth, the sea, and all that in them is, and rested the seventh day: *wherefore the Lord blessed the sabbath day, and hallowed it.*"   Exodus 20:8-11

Especially His Tithe

"*Will a man rob God? Yet ye have robbed me.* But ye say, Wherein have we robbed thee? *In tithes and offerings.* . . . Bring ye all the tithes into the storehouse, that there may be meat in mine house, and prove me now herewith, saith the Lord of hosts, if I will not open you the windows of heaven, and pour you out a blessing, that there shall not be room enough to receive it."　　Malachi 3:8, 10

Put Others Before Yourself

Jesus said: "Therefore all things *whatsoever ye would that men should do to you, do ye even so to them:* for this is the law and the prophets."
Matthew 7:12

The Apostle Paul said: "Let nothing be done through strife or vainglory; but *in lowliness of mind let each esteem other better than themselves.* Look not every man on his own things, but every man also on the things of others."　　Philippians 2:3, 4

Be Clean In Everything You Do

In Thought

"Finally, brethren, *whatsoever things are true, whatsoever things are honest, whatsoever things are just, whatsoever things are pure, whatsoever things are lovely, whatsoever things are of good report;* if there be any virtue, and if there by any praise, *think on these things.*"
Philippians 4:8

In Conversation

"Seeing then that all these things shall be dissolved, *what manner of persons ought ye to be in all holy conversation and godliness.*"　　2 Peter 3:11

In Deportment (your behavior)

"*He that saith he abideth in him ought himself also so to walk, even as he walked. . .* And every man that hath this hope in him purifieth himself, even as he is pure."   1 John 2:6 & 3:3

In Your Body

"*What? know ye not that your body is the temple of the Holy Ghost* which is in you, which ye have of God, and ye are not your own?" "*If any man defile the temple of God, him shall God destroy;* for the temple of God is holy, which temple ye are." "For ye are bought with a price: *therefore glorify God in your body,* and in your spirit, which are God's."   1 Corinthians 6:19; 3:17; 6:20

"*For thou art a holy people unto the Lord thy God,* and the Lord hath chosen thee to be a peculiar people unto himself, above all the nations that are upon the earth. *Thou shalt not eat any abominable thing.*"   Deuteronomy 14:2, 3

In Your Dress and Adornment

"Then Jacob said unto his household, and to all that were with him, Put away the strange gods that are among you, and *be clean, and change your garments. . . And they gave unto Jacob all the strange gods which were in their hand, and all their earrings which were in their ears;* and Jacob hid them under the oak which was by She-chem."   Genesis 35:2, 4

"*I also want women to dress modestly, with decency and propriety, not with braided hair or gold or pearls or expensive clothes,* but with good deeds, appropriate for women who profess to worship God"   1 Timothy 2:9 *(New International Version)*

*"Whose adorning let it not be that outward
adorning of plaiting the hair, and of wearing
of gold, or of putting on of apparel; But let it
be the hidden man of the heart,* in that which is
not corruptible, even the ornament of a meek and quiet
spirit, which is in the sight of God of great price."

1 Peter 3:3, 4

Be Prudent In Your Finances

Owe no man any thing, but to love one another:
for he that loveth another hath fulfilled the law.

Romans 13:8

Seek The Fellowship Of Believers

"And let us consider how we may spur one another on
toward love and good deeds. *Let us not give up
meeting together, as some are in the habit of
doing,* but let us encourage one another - and all the
more as you see the Day approaching."

Hebrews 10:24, 25 NIV *(New International Version)*

Surrender Everything To Christ

"And he said to them all, *If any man will come
after me, let him deny himself, and take up his
cross daily, and follow me."*   Luke 9:23

*"Then answered Peter and said unto him,
Behold, we have forsaken all, and followed
thee; what shall we have therefore? . . .* And
every one that hath forsaken houses, or brethren, or
sisters, or father, or mother, or wife, or children, or lands,
for my name's sake, shall receive an hundredfold, and shall
inherit everlasting life."   Matthew 19:27, 29

Share Christ With Others

"Go ye therefore, and teach all nations, baptizing them in the name of the Father, and of the Son, and of the Holy Ghost: Teaching them to observe all things whatsoever I have commanded you: and, lo, I am with you alway, even unto the end of the world. Amen."   Matthew 28:19, 20

Keep God's Commandments

"Blessed are they that do his commandments, that they may have right to the tree of life, and may enter in through the gates into the city."   Revelation 22:14

"Let us hear the conclusion of the whole matter: Fear God, and keep his commandments: for this is the whole duty of man. For God shall bring every work into judgment, with every secret thing, whether it be good, or whether it be evil."

Ecclesiastes 12:13, 14